PRINCIPLES OF POSSE MANAGEMENT

Lessons from the Old West for Today's Leaders

CHRIS ENSS

TWODOT®

GUILFORD, CONNECTICUT
HELENA, MONTANA

A · TWODOT® · BOOK

An imprint of The Rowman & Littlefield Publishing Group, Inc.
4501 Forbes Blvd., Ste. 200
Lanham, MD 20706
www.rowman.com
A registered trademark of The Rowman & Littlefield Publishing Group, Inc.

Distributed by NATIONAL BOOK NETWORK

British Library Cataloguing in Publication Information available

Library of Congress Cataloging-in-Publication Data available

ISBN 978-1-4930-2553-4 (paperback)
ISBN 978-1-4930-2554-1 (e-book)

∞™ The paper used in this publication meets the minimum requirements of American National Standard for Information Sciences—Permanence of Paper for Printed Library Materials, ANSI/NISO Z39.48-1992.

Printed in the United States of America

For the boys in my Bible study class, who bring me joy each week:

Jeffrey, Josh, Jessie, Austin, Corbin, Daniel, Zac, David, Dominick, Dorian, Joey, R.J., Evan, Ian, and Ethan

CONTENTS

ACKNOWLEDGMENTS

With a deep sense of gratitude, the author expresses her appreciation for the help given her by a large number of valuable organizations and interested men and women, among them being:

Arizona Historical Society
Kathleen Correia at the California State Library
Denver Public Library
Indiana Historical Society
Kansas State Historical Society
New Mexico Commission of Public Records
Oklahoma Historical Society
Texas Ranger Hall of Fame
Author and historian John Boessenecker
Erin Turner and the editors, graphic artists, and promotional staff
    members at TwoDot.

INTRODUCTION

In nearly every Western film prior to 1950, you'll find a sheriff hastily assembling a group of men to track down an outlaw or two. Area ranchers, or whoever was in the saloon after a shooting in the middle of the street, were quickly deputized. The posse would then mount their horses and take off in search of the bad guys.

No one asked if the posse members could shoot straight, if they had their own guns and ammunition, or if they'd had experience hunting fugitives. Questions weren't posed about how long they could stay in the saddle or how long they could be away from their homes, farms, or businesses. It would appear all that was needed was a collection of outraged citizens. Exactly what went into forming an effective posse was much more refined than motion pictures presented.

The original term for posse was *posse comitatus*, taken from the Latin, meaning the "force of the country." Any law officer could order anyone to help him "keep the peace" or to chase and arrest a felon. People who wouldn't help do that were fined.[1]

The history of sheriffs forming posses began in Anglo-Saxon England. The word *sheriff* is a combination of the Anglo-Saxon words for "shire" (what today we call a "county") and "reeve" (meaning "guardian"). Those who guarded English counties were responsible for organizing communal defense.[2]

COURTESY OF THE LIBRARY OF CONGRESS

Forty-seven lawmen made up the posse after Mexican
warlord-turned-outlaw, Colonel Pascual Orozco.

According to David Kopel, a law professor from Denver University, the office of sheriff in England was declining by the time the American colonies were being settled. The office had a resurgence in popularity once the colonies were solidified. It was decided then that the law enforcement agent would be elected to the position by popular vote. "The Americans also strongly reaffirmed the traditional common law understanding of the sheriff's powers and authorities, especially the sheriff's autonomy and independence," Professor Kopel noted in a *Washington Post* article from May 15, 2014. "During the latter nineteenth century, elections and other common law principles were often formally constitutionalized in the new states. Legally speaking, the Office of Sheriff in most states has changed little since the nineteenth century."[3]

Since the inception of the office, the sheriff has had the authority to summon a posse. Posse service is a mandatory duty of the citizen, and he must respond. The ability to organize a posse is not limited to the sheriff's office, however. Justices of the peace, judges, and marshals also have the authority.[4]

With few exceptions, posses were generally small in size. As many as forty-seven people might have been assembled to take part in a posse, as in the case of the posse that tracked the Mexican revolutionary leader and warlord-turned-outlaw named Pascual Orozco Vazquez in 1915.[5]

Texas sheriff William Davis Allison, the youngest sheriff in Texas history, was in charge of the large group of men mandated to apprehend Orozco. In order to best do the job, Sheriff Allison divided the band into smaller segments. He felt the posse could cover more territory and were less likely to be seen by the renegades they were chasing in parties of only four or five men.[6]

Sheriff Allison's posse tracked Orozco over a 120-mile area of the state of Texas. The pursuit ended in Culberson County, two miles from the base of High Lonesome Mountain. Orozco and four of his fellow outlaws refused to give themselves up and be arrested. The bandits were shot and killed when they opened fire on law enforcement.[7]

There were rare occasions when a combined effort of more than one hundred men was enlisted to track an escaped desperado. In 1856, cattle rustler, horse thief, and robber of stages Juan Flores was riding roughshod over a territory that extended from Sacramento to the San Joaquin Valley. An initial posse of six men headed by Los Angeles sheriff James R.

Bass Reeves was a deputy US marshal for more than thirty-five years and captured numerous outlaws. He was a one-man posse.

Barton rode to an area outside San Juan Capistrano where Flores was last seen. Their job was to arrest the outlaw and escort him to jail. The lawmen were not successful. Flores and his gang shot and killed the officers, stripped them of their belongings, and cut out their right eyes.[8]

The bandit's crime was considered so egregious and offensive that General Don Andres Pico, a prominent Los Angeles landowner and brother of the last Mexican governor of California, took charge of forming a posse. Pico pulled together a fifty-one-man army of Mexicans and Americans to go after Flores. Pauma Indian leader Manuelito

Dodge City's Chalk Beeson was a welcome member of many posses.

Cota in Temecula joined the general in his efforts, recruiting forty-three Indians for the task. A group of enraged citizens in the San Diego area made up a third posse out to track Flores.[9]

Pauma scouts ventured ahead of the posse to look for clues as to where the bandit might have fled. The location of Flores's camp was finally narrowed down to the mountains around El Cariso. With the assistance of one of Flores's former gang members, Pico's Californians, as the posse was known, were able to find the exact location of Flores's cabin hideout. The Californians attacked the shelter under the light of a full moon. The desperadoes inside fired on the posse, killing or wounding many of their pursuers. Some of the bandits were shot while trying to make a run for their horses; others were captured unharmed, and some managed to get away. Juan Flores and his outlaw partner Andres Fontes were two who escaped.[10]

Flores and Fontes were lost in the smoke of gunfire and vanished into the tangled mountain thicket. General Pico sent for reinforcements, and shortly after his supplies of guns, ammunition, and men were replenished, he continued the pursuit of the outlaws. On February 1, 1857, a faction of the posse, headed by Dr. J. Gentry from Los Angeles, cornered Flores and two of his companions near Santiago Mountain.[11]

The bandits shot it out with the posse members, but, realizing they were outnumbered, they eventually surrendered. Flores and his diminished band of followers were escorted to a nearby ranch where they were placed under guard in a weathered adobe building. The prisoners' stay was meant to be temporary. Given Flores's previous success at escaping from his captors, the authorities wanted more law enforcement on hand to escort the criminal to the Los Angeles jail. Despite the precautions taken, Flores wriggled from his cuffs and escaped the crumbling, clay holding cell.[12]

Posse members' tempers flared at the news that Flores had gotten away. General Pico ordered his deputies to immediately put to death the members of Flores's gang that had been arrested with him. Pico then helped to enlist more than 120 men to join the manhunt to find Juan Flores once again. For eleven days, one of the largest posses ever assembled in the Old West searched the territory along the Los Angeles River between San Juan Capistrano and Temecula.[13]

Almost twenty-four hours after Flores had escaped, he was stopped by two armed sentinels patrolling the grounds at a Simi Valley ranch. He lied about his identity, but his suspicious behavior led the guards to take him to the ranch owner to be questioned further. The land baron recognized the bandit and informed his men that the scoundrel in custody was none other than Juan Flores.[14]

Bandits outside Leadville, Colorado, wait to rob a stage. No doubt a posse was after them not long after the crime was committed.

Flores was taken to Los Angeles where he was tried and sentenced to death. After his trial ended on February 14, 1857, a hostile crowd surrounded the jail, demanding the notorious outlaw be turned over to them. They wanted Flores hanged at that moment. On February 21, the criminal was turned over to the enraged mob, and they led him to the gallows.[15]

Before the noose was placed around his neck, the twenty-two-year-old Flores's arms and legs were bound, and his eyes were covered with a white handkerchief. He whispered a few last words, and then the trapdoor was sprung. He did not die instantly. The fall was shorter than planned, and the rope was a bit too long. After a gruesome, six-minute struggle, it was over.[16]

Temple Lea Houston, son of Sam Houston, was a skilled gunman who was often sought to join or lead a posse.

Posse organizers, determined to bring in a suspect no matter what, made sure to recruit those who were proficient with a firearm. Tennessee native Commodore Perry Owens's skill with a gun was renowned in the Arizona Territory in 1881. Between 1882 and 1886, when he was elected sheriff of Apache County, Arizona, he was often called on to be a part of a posse because he was such an exceptional shot. Perry and a handful of others were hired by the government to find three Navajo Indians who had left the reservation and driven off-range cattle in the Navajo Springs area. The skilled gunman located the Indians who were trying to start a stampede. Perry stopped the men cold when they tried to rush him together. All three were shot dead.[17]

The reputation he gained from this incident helped earn him a permanent spot on any posse put together in southwest Arizona and an appointment as sheriff.

Temple Lea Houston, the son of Sam Houston, was another skilled gunman who was often sought to join or lead a posse. Temple was a criminal attorney by trade who was as well-known for his expertise with a pistol as he was for his physical appearance. His shoulder-length hair was often covered with a white sombrero, and he always wore rattlesnake ties.[18]

Houston wasn't only asked to join a posse because he was good with a gun, but also because he knew the law. It was essential that state- and local government–sanctioned posses adhered to the law. Unless otherwise specified, a posse was required to arrest a fugitive and escort him to jail where he would await trial. Elected officials and community leaders believed the only way to tame the Wild West was to bring about law and order. Apprehending lawbreakers and making them work within the guidelines of the court system demonstrated to the public at large that there was a civilized way to see justice done.

Those recruited to be a part of a successful sheriff's posse were selected because the law enforcement agent knew they would excel at the job even though they might not get paid for doing it. Payment depended on the government body involved, but, for the most part, volunteers received no pay. Serving on a posse was viewed no differently than serving on a jury: It was your civic duty. If a reward was paid for apprehending an outlaw, the sheriff or marshal would usually share it with his possemen, but there were no guarantees.[19]

There was no way to determine from the outset how long a posse would need to ride before they captured a suspect or suspects. Posse

AUTHOR'S COLLECTION

A posse out of Texas poses for a photograph in 1879.

members had to be able to commit to long rides if necessary. Recruits who were not law enforcement officers were often selected based on how easily they could leave their businesses.

Dodge City, Kansas, resident Chalk Beeson was always willing to take part in a posse. Not only did he own the Long Branch Saloon, but he was also a cattle rancher. He could take time away from both enterprises because he had partners who managed affairs in his absence. Beeson decided to sell the saloon in 1883 and was elected sheriff of Ford County, Kansas, in 1891.[20]

Men who were acutely familiar with the area where a posse was called on to track an outlaw were invaluable. It was also considered a plus if they were willing to change their appearance to acquire infor-

ALVIN RUCKER COLLECTION, OKLAHOMA HISTORICAL SOCIETY

Posse out of Medicine Lodge, Kansas, in 1932.

mation about where the bad guys might be hiding. Deputy US Marshal Bass Reeves was a benefit to any posse because he was an expert tracker and wasn't too proud to alter his looks in order to ensure an arrest.[21]

Born a slave in 1838, Reeves lived in Paris, Texas, for a number of years before fleeing slavery to live among the Indians in what is now Oklahoma. He was a giant of a man, standing over six feet tall. His look was made all the more imposing because of the black hat he wore upturned in the front. He was an expert with the twin Colts he wore on his hips, and he never backed down from a challenge. According to the January 2, 1907, edition of the *Daily Ardmoreite*, Reeves was known as a "terror to the black outlaws and bootleggers." He had a reputation for never failing to capture a man he went after, bringing them in, dead or alive.[22]

Reeves was living in Van Buren, Arkansas, when US Marshal James Fagan suggested Judge Isaac Parker hire him to be a marshal. The Indian Territory was being overrun with thieves and murderers, and lawmen were needed to police the area and keep it safe. He was an expert on the terrain and could speak several Native American languages. Reeves served for thirty-five years as a deputy US marshal. He covered seventy-five thousand square miles and captured more than three thousand criminals, killing fourteen.[23]

Reeves was handy with a disguise should the situation call for it. On one occasion, he dressed as a down-and-out hobo in search of food and shelter in order to arrest three known highwaymen. Pretending to be on the run from the law himself, Reeves traveled to the home of the bandits and talked his way inside. The unsuspecting men were arrested for their crimes, and Reeves then marched them twenty-eight miles to jail. The outlaws were locked up and Reeves collected a $5,000 reward.[24]

Throughout his long and accomplished career, Reeves tracked down a number of ruthless criminals, such as cattle rustler Tom Story and bank robber Bob Dozier, but no desperado proved to be as difficult for Reeves to apprehend as his own son. In a violent rage, Reeves's oldest son, Benjamin, beat his wife to death. The young Reeves then fled to Indian Territory. Two weeks after receiving the arrest warrant, Bass returned with his son in tow. Benjamin was tried for murder, found guilty, and sentenced to life in prison at Fort Leavenworth, Kansas.[25]

Few probably think of lawmen such as Bass Reeves, Heck Thomas, and Bat Masterson as management experts, but solid management skills were the key to quickly organizing law enforcement officers to keep the peace and pursue and arrest felons. The most accomplished and legendary manhunts of the Old West were organized using a set of

C. B. RHODES COLLECTION, OKLAHOMA HISTORICAL SOCIETY

The posse that captured criminal Ned Christie.

standards or principles that can be employed in business today. What posses—such as the one that left Dodge City, Kansas, in 1878 to track the killer of dance-hall singer and actress Dora Hand—have to teach is applicable in current corporate settings.[26]

In the chapters that follow, you'll find examples of how the most unlikely management teams helped bring order to the chaotic Western frontier. *Principles of Posse Management* is all about how to best assemble a focused group of individuals and continue on smoothly and efficiently toward the completion of a task.

Let's ride.

Management Principles Learned from the Posse after the Reno Gang

Identify your objective and carefully consider how you want to hit your target.

Allan Pinkerton was able to track the bandits responsible for robbing the Adams Express Company only after he was given a full description of the Reno gang members. That basic information led the posse to the outlaws' hiding place, where they could put together a plan to apprehend the bad guys and retrieve the stolen money.

Go the extra mile.

When the Pinkerton posse kidnapped the leader of the Reno gang, they were employing extreme measures to ensure that the desperadoes faced justice. That daring action proved to be positive for the detective agency because businesses could see that the Pinkertons offered exceptional service. Allan Pinkerton and his men were hired to solve several other robberies after bringing in the Reno gang.

Never underestimate the powers of observation.

If the posse hadn't been paying close attention to the comings and goings of various townspeople in Council Bluffs, Iowa, they would have missed the strange behavior of a citizen who eventually led them to the spot where the Reno gang was hiding.

Embrace the benefits of cross training.

Posse members took on a variety jobs in an effort to achieve their objective. Some worked as bartenders, others as railroad employees. They gained valuable knowledge about the offenders they were after that helped to define the best way to apprehend the Renos.

Follow a job to the end.

You haven't failed until you quit trying. The Pinkerton posse never abandoned their quest to arrest the Reno gang, even when the outlaws fled to Canada. The bandits thought they were safe in another country, but Pinkerton acquired the necessary legal documents to have them extradited.

CHAPTER ONE

You Haven't Failed until You Quit Trying: The Posse after the Reno Gang

Newspaper readers from Hartford, Connecticut, to Portland, Oregon, were shocked to read about the bold and daring robbery of the Ohio and Mississippi Railroad on October 6, 1866. It was the first robbery of its kind. Banks and stage lines had been robbed before, but no one had perpetrated such a crime on a railroad. According to the October 20, 1866, edition of the *Altoona Tribune*, three masked bandits entered the car stopped at a station near Seymour, Indiana, with the idea of taking money from the Adams Express safe. They entered the car from the front platform, leveled their revolvers at the head of the guard on duty, and demanded he hand over the keys to the safe. He did so with no argument.[1]

While one of the bandits stood guard, the others opened and removed the contents of one of the three safes which included more than $20,000 in cash. When the job was done, the desperadoes moved one of the safes to the door of the car, opened it, and tossed the box out. The heavy safe hit the ground hard, rolled, and came to a stop. One of the masked men pulled on the bell cord, and, as the engineer replied with the signal to apply the brakes, the robbers jumped out of the train and made their escape.[2]

The engineer saw the bandits leap off the train and speculated they were headed in the direction of Seymour. The train slowed to a stop and one of the agents for the Adams Express Company who was on the train hopped off and ran back to the station with the news of the robbery. He commandeered a handcar and recruited a few men to help him collect any evidence left behind by the thieves. On the agent's way back to the train, he found the safe tossed from the car. The $15,000 inside had not been touched.[3]

The Adams Express Company offered a $5,000 reward for the arrest and conviction of the robbers. A witness aboard the train the evening it was robbed told authorities he recognized the desperadoes who stole the money as the Reno brothers, John and Simeon, and one of their friends, Frank Sparks. Citizens and detectives alike began a vigorous search, but the brothers proved impossible to locate.[4]

Unbeknownst to the Reno boys and the gang of outlaws with whom they associated, the Pinkerton Detective Agency had been hired to protect all Adams Express Company shipments. Armed with the descriptions provided by the witness, Allan Pinkerton, head of the investigation firm, set out to find the culprits. Pinkerton traced the Renos to Seymour, a lawless community where rustlers, bandits, and cutthroats from all over the area gathered.[5]

The history of the Renos in Seymour, Indiana, dates back to 1813. Prior to living in Indiana, the Reno clan had settled in Kentucky. Five boys and one girl were born to William and Julia Ann. William was a farmer and tried to teach his sons about how to work the land. The boys preferred gambling and stealing horses over honest labor. No amount of discipline could keep the boys focused. A news report in the July 20, 1868, edition of the *Vermont Daily Transcript* noted that the Reno boys' bad behavior drove William to insanity. Julia Ann filed for divorce shortly after local authorities deemed it necessary for a guardian to watch over William on a continual basis to keep him from harming himself.[6]

In 1861, Frank Reno and his friend Frank Sparks both fought in the Civil War as Union soldiers. John Reno enlisted in the Indianapolis Grays, but deserted before the end of his term. With the exception of the youngest Reno boy, Clinton, all made a substantial amount of money as bounty jumpers. Wealthy men who were drafted to fight in the war against the state would hire someone to take their place for a fee. The Reno boys would accept the bounty and enlist using another's name, desert, and repeat the process.[7]

In addition to being bounty jumpers, the boys broke into homes and stores and stole money and merchandise. By early 1866, the Renos had made a name for themselves as thieves and cheats. They inducted a number of other dishonest individuals into their fold, including counterfeiters and safe burglars. Their influence extended to politicians and prominent citizens, too. Making charges stick after they were arrested for their crimes was impossible. The Renos had become such a powerful force, no one dared go against them for fear of reprisal.[8]

The Reno brothers became bored with the customary acts of violence and local thievery. Their desire to steal on a grand scale led them to consider robbing trains. Allan Pinkerton recruited a posse of operatives who could pass themselves off as bandits looking to join the Reno gang. One of Pinkerton's operatives, Dick Winscott, infiltrated a saloon in Seymour pretending to be the new owner of the establishment. Winscott and the other agents then waited for the boys to come around. In a short time, the agents knew the exact location of the key members of the group, and authorities moved in to arrest the bandits and hold them over for trial for train robbery. On October 11, 1866, the Renos made bail and were released. The one witness who had identified the boys at the train holdup was found dead from a gunshot wound. The law maintained that without a witness there was no case against the Renos. The charges against them were dismissed.[9]

Other train robberies followed in quick succession, the same methods used in each one, with the same immunity from capture. People in the region were saying to one another, quite as a matter of course: "The Reno brothers got away with another train robbery yesterday."[10]

The Renos' ability to intimidate the area in and around Seymour gave them the idea they were untouchable. Feeling invincible, they pushed their raids beyond Indiana into Illinois and Missouri. They galloped across the country leaving a trail of busted safes and murdered men behind them. The gang of highwaymen and murderers were territorial as well. Any lawbreakers outside their group were harshly dealt with. More than a year after the first train robbery was perpetrated, two men named Walker Hammond and Michael Colleran robbed an Ohio and Mississippi train outside Seymour, escaping with $8,000. The robbery was so similar in time and location to the first time the Ohio and Mississippi was robbed that the crime was blamed on the Renos. Furious that they were being targeted for a robbery they had no part in, the Reno gang set out to clear their names. The Reno brothers tracked Hammond and Colleran down, gave them severe beatings, and turned them over to the authorities. The two men were quickly indicted for robbery and later sentenced to a combined eleven years in prison.[11]

While Hammond and Colleran were paying their debt to society for robbing the Ohio and Mississippi, John Reno was leading his brothers and other members of his gang on a raid of the Davies County Treasury in Gallatin, Missouri. The robbery occurred on November 17, 1867. The outlaws stole more than $22,000. The county treasury was not protected by the Pinkerton Agency, but that didn't stop the general manager of the Adams Express Company from contacting Allan Pinkerton to investigate the matter.[12]

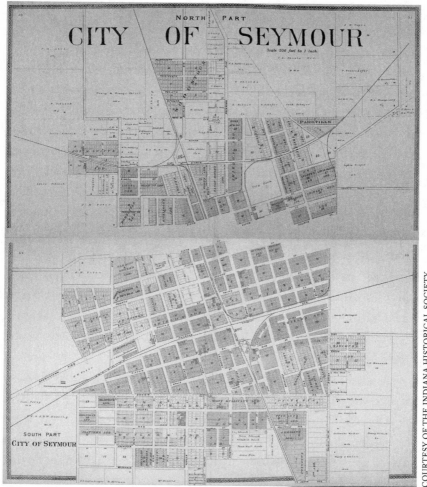

Map of Seymour, Indiana, site of America's first planned train robbery.

Sixteen years prior to the Renos robbing the Ohio and Mississippi Railroad, Pinkerton had opened the world's first private detective agency in Chicago. Police forces were often poorly staffed in the mid-1860s in the West, and sometimes there were no police at all. Allan Pinkerton's agency was called upon for a great variety of police tasks. His operatives chased and captured bandits, bank robbers, and train robbers all over the country. Pinkerton knew the Reno brothers were responsible for the train robbery in October 1866. Witnesses or no, he was going to pursue the Renos, arrest them for their actions, and recover the money stolen from the Adams Express Company. He was grateful that company executives were giving him a second chance to apprehend the outlaws.[13]

Pinkerton agents in Missouri gathered enough evidence to prove the Renos stole the money from the treasury in Gallatin. Pinkerton sent word to Dick Winscott and the other operatives in Seymour to ask about the outlaws' activities and to discuss what action should be taken. All agreed that any attempt by the Pinkertons to ride into Seymour to take John Reno and his brother would most assuredly result in a gun battle, with innocent lives endangered.[14]

Pinkerton discussed the situation with his staff in Chicago. It was decided the only way to get the Renos to face justice was by kidnapping their leader, John Reno. Pinkerton and the others agreed that the end justified the means.

Allan Pinkerton sent a wire to the sheriff of Davies County to meet him in Cincinnati with a writ for the Indiana outlaw. Pinkerton then traveled from Chicago to Cincinnati and boarded a special train he had hired. Six additional Pinkerton operatives accompanied him. Pinkerton sent word to Winscott to somehow get John Reno to the depot platform at a specific time. Two days after the plan was conceived, Winscott sent a wire to Pinkerton to let him know he would have John on the platform at the designated hour. The outlaw suspected nothing.

He thought he was going to meet a friend. As the train pulled into Seymour, Pinkerton spotted Winscott laughing and talking with John Reno. Pinkerton and his men exited the train with the other passengers and casually surrounded the outlaw on all sides. Their movements were so fluid John wasn't aware of what was going on. He tried to escape, but he was quickly overpowered and his arms pulled behind him. John was forced onto the train and into a private car where he was handcuffed and tied with rope. Pinkerton then signaled to the engineer to start the train moving on its way.[15]

As soon as the other members of the Reno gang learned what had happened, they gathered in force to stop the train. Try as they might, they couldn't catch up with the vehicle, and the chase was abandoned.

John Reno was brought before a judge in Gallatin the following day. The judge was stern and informed the bandit that if he didn't return the money he had stolen from the county treasurer's office, he would be hanged. John was placed in a jail cell, and several guards kept watch over him twenty-four hours a day, seven days a week. Word of Reno's arrest spread throughout the countryside, and armed victims of the Reno gang's crimes made their ways to the jail to deal with the outlaw personally. On January 18, 1868, John was escorted to the Indiana Penitentiary in Michigan City where he would be better protected from vigilantes.[16]

While John was safely locked in prison, his brothers and other Reno gang members robbed the county treasurer's office at Magnolia in Harrison County, Iowa, of $14,000. Pinkerton was again called in to investigate in early March 1868. He arrived at the scene of the crime with his son William and two other operatives, just the right number of people needed to track down and capture the Renos.[17]

The Pinkerton agents determined that the Renos had fled Harrison County with the money on a railroad handcar and that they had gone in the direction of Council Bluffs. One of the saloons in Council Bluffs was operated by a man who had lived in Seymour, Indiana, and knew the Reno brothers personally. Pinkerton and his cohorts figured that the outlaws would end up there. He and his men hurried to Council Bluffs to survey the town and wait for the Renos.[18]

After two days spent watching, the detectives observed a large man of dark complexion enter the saloon and engage in close conversation with the proprietor. Further investigation revealed the man to be Michael Rogers, a prominent and wealthy citizen of Council Bluffs and the owner of extensive property in the adjoining counties. Puzzled but still persuaded he had found a clue, Pinkerton put a "shadow" on Rogers and hurried back to Magnolia, where Rogers paid his taxes and hung around the treasurer's office for most of the day. The Pinkerton operatives thought Rogers's behavior was suspicious, but all the background investigation on Rogers showed he was a respectable businessman. Pinkerton wasn't convinced that Rogers was as upstanding as initial reports noted. He conferred with Rogers's shadow, who informed him that several strange men had been seen entering Rogers's house, but had not been seen coming out again.[19]

Pinkerton now joined the shadow watching Rogers. After four days of patiently waiting, Rogers, accompanied by three strangers, was seen leaving the house and heading to the depot. They then took a west-bound train on the Pacific Railroad. Pinkerton shrewdly suspected that one of the men, a brawny, athletic fellow nearly six feet tall and about twenty-eight years of age, was Frank Reno. Feeling sure that if his suspicions were correct, the men would ultimately return to Rogers's house, Pinkerton did not follow them on the train but contented himself with keeping the strictest watch for their return. The very next morning, the same four men were discovered coming back to Rogers's house from the direction of the railroad. There were no trains due at that time of day, which was a little curious; another curious point was that they were all covered with mud and bore marks of having been engaged in some severe, rough labor.[20]

Close to noon, Council Bluffs was abuzz with the news that the safe of the county treasurer at Glenwood in Mills County, about thirty miles away, had been robbed the previous night. There were no traces of the thieves, but everything indicated they were the same men who had robbed the safe at Magnolia. One remarkable point of similarity in the two cases was the means employed by the robbers in escaping: A handcar was also used by the Glenwood thieves to get away. They, too, were believed to have fled in the direction of Council Bluffs. Investigation soon made this absolutely certain, for the missing handcar was found lying beside the railroad a short distance from the Council Bluffs station.[21]

Putting these new disclosures beside his previous suspicions and discoveries, Pinkerton was further strengthened in his distrust of the man Rogers. He resolved to attempt an arrest, although the local authorities, to whom he revealed his suspicions, laughed at him and declared that Rogers was one of the most respectable citizens of the state. According to an account of the incident found in the Pinkerton archives, Pinkerton proceeded to Rogers's house with all the force he could command; he placed a guard at the front and rear, and then, with a few attendants, made his way inside.

The first person he met was Rogers himself, indignant at the intrusion.[22]

"Who have you in this house?" Pinkerton asked.

"Nobody but my family," answered Rogers.

"We'll see about that," retorted Pinkerton. Then, turning to his men, he ordered them to search the premises.[23]

They did so, and soon came upon the three strangers, who were so completely taken by surprise that they made no attempt to flee. They were about to sit down to breakfast, laid out for them in the kitchen. One of the men was Frank Reno. A second, a man of dark complexion, tall, and well built, proved to be Albert Perkins, a well-known member of the Reno gang. The third was none other than the notorious Miles Ogle, the youngest member of the band, who afterwards came to be known as the most expert counterfeiter in the United States.[24]

While they were securing the four men, the detectives noticed that smoke was curling out of the kitchen stove, accompanied by a sudden blaze. Pinkerton pulled off a lid and found on the coals several packages of banknotes already on fire. Fortunately, the notes had been so tightly wrapped together that only a few of them were destroyed before the fire was put out. Those that remained were afterwards identified as of the money that had been stolen from the Glenwood safe. There was then no question that these were the long-sought robbers. A further search of the house brought to light two sets of burglars' tools, which served as cumulative evidence.[25]

The men were taken to Glenwood on the next train. They were met by a great and excited crowd, and for a time were in danger of being lynched. Better counsel prevailed, however, and they were placed in the jail to await trial. The Reno gang could not be contained, and on April 1, 1868, the outlaws escaped from jail. A rudimentary saw had been used to cut out a giant hole in the wall where the criminals made their getaway. The words "April Fool" had been scrawled in chalk on the floors and walls of the jail.[26]

A large reward was offered for the capture of the robbers, but nothing was heard of them until two months later, when an express car on the Ohio and Mississippi Railroad was boarded at Marshfield, Indiana, by a gang of masked men and robbed of $98,000. The messenger put up a good fight but could not cope with the robbers, who lifted him bodily and hurled him out of the car and down a steep embankment while the train was running at high speed.[27]

All the facts in the case pointed to the Reno brothers as the authors of this outrage, for, by frequent repetition, their methods of robbery had become familiar. Pinkerton, furthermore, obtained precise evidence from secret agents, whom he had stationed at Seymour to watch the doings of the gang, confirming that it was the work of the Renos. Two of these agents engaged in business at Seymour, one setting up as a saloon keeper in a rough part of town and another taking a job with the railroad, which kept him constantly near the station. A third agent passed himself off as a gambler. So successful were they that Pinkerton was soon in possession of facts proving not only that the Marshfield robbery had been committed by the Renos, but also that another train robbery which followed was executed by John Moore, Charles Gerroll, William Sparks, and three others, all members of the Reno organization.[28]

Pinkerton and five operatives, including Dick Winscott, made up the posse that rode into Coles County, Illinois, to search the countryside for the train robbers. It had been rumored that some of the gang fled to that area after their last holdup. Frank Reno, Charlie Anderson, Albert Perkins, Michael Rogers, and Miles Ogle escaped to Canada; Simeon and William Reno hid out in Minneapolis; Sparks, Gerroll, and Moore were the ones in Coles County, Illinois. The Pinkerton posse found and arrested the trio. They were loaded onto a train bound for Indianapolis in the same baggage car they had robbed, still full of bullet holes.

None of the three would make it to their destination.[29]

The train made numerous, seemingly unnecessary stops en route to Indiana. Each time the curious Pinkerton men would watch the engineer jump from his cab and inspect the wheels or engine. It was as though the journey was being purposefully slowed. Pinkerton and the other operatives suspected something was going to happen involving the gang members in custody. Vigilante groups had threatened to intercept the transportation of the outlaws. Pinkerton questioned the engineer about the frequent stops and was told the train was in need of repairs. He was insistent that he needed to closely monitor the wheels and other parts to ensure a safe arrival. It was 10:30 at night when the train came to yet another stop three miles outside Seymour. Nervous that either a pro-Reno force or an anti-Reno mob would seize the moment to overtake the detectives, Pinkerton decided to offload their horses from the livestock car and haul the prisoners on to Brownstown on horseback.[30]

The Pinkerton posse was barely on its way when more than two hundred men wearing crimson flannel masks rose out of the bushes and overpowered the detectives. The Pinkerton detectives were ordered to surrender their weapons and their rides and to start walking back toward Coles County. The masked men seized the outlaws and carried them away to a nearby farmyard and hanged them from a beech tree.[31]

This was the first act of retribution justice committed by the Secret Vigilance Committee of Southern Indiana. The entire population of that part of Indiana seemed to have risen in self-defense to crush lawlessness. A second act followed several days later, when three other men who had been implicated in the latest train robbery, having been captured by the county officials, were taken from custody and condemned to the same fate as their companions. Each one, as he was about to be swung off, was asked by the mask-wearing vigilantes if he had anything to say. The first two shook their heads sullenly and died without speaking. The third, standing on a barrel with the rope around his neck, looked over the crowd with contemptuous bravado and, addressing them as a lot of "mossback Hoosiers," said he was glad he was not of

COURTESY OF THE LIBRARY OF CONGRESS

Allan Pinkerton.

their class and pronounced he was proud to die as a good Republican. The barrel was kicked away. The rope stiffened with his weight, and there ended the career of the sixth member of the Reno gang.[32]

The race was now on between the Pinkertons and the Secret Vigilance Committee of Southern Indiana as to who would first reach the Reno gang members still at large. The vigilantes were serious about their quest and openly campaigned for funds for a war chest to hang the Renos publicly when and if they were captured.[33]

William and Simeon Reno were arrested by Pinkerton operative William Stiggart on July 22, 1868, in Indianapolis. The outlaws were turned over to the local authorities, who transported the prisoners to New Albany in Floyd County, Indiana, to keep them safe from the

Vigilance Committee. Pinkerton detectives continued to track down Reno gang members who had escaped the Glenwood jail. They found Miles Ogle and Albert Perkins in Indianapolis. Frank Reno was discovered in Windsor, Canada. He was living with Charlie Anderson, a professional gambler, who had fled to Canada to escape prosecution. Frank Reno, operating with Anderson, made a practice of registering as "Frank Going" if the enterprise in which he was engaged was prospering, and as "Frank Coming" if it was not prospering. He and Anderson were now arrested on a charge of robbery and of assault with intent to kill, in the case of the express messenger hurled from his car at Marshfield, Indiana. The men were ordered for extradition. Aided by the ablest lawyers, however, they carried their case to the highest court in Canada. The decision of the lower court was affirmed, and in October 1868, they were surrendered into the hands of Pinkerton, who had been delegated by the United States government to receive them.[34]

Michael Rogers was also discovered to be in Windsor at this time, and he was known to have had a hand in the Marshfield robbery. He escaped arrest and remained securely in Windsor for a year or two. He was eventually placed in the penitentiary for a robbery in Tolono, Illinois. When he was released, he joined the notorious McCartney gang of counterfeiters and had many narrow escapes. The last known of him was that he had lived to be an old man and was residing quietly on a farm in Texas.[35]

Pinkerton chartered a tug to carry Frank Reno and Charlie Anderson to Cleveland, and thereby avoid the friends who, as he had reason to know, were waiting across the river in Detroit to try and rescue the outlaws. When the tug had gone about twenty miles, it was run down by a large steamer and sunk, the passengers, including the prisoners, being saved from drowning with the greatest difficulty. The prisoners were carried to Cleveland by another boat and from there were hurried on by rail to New Albany, where they were placed in jail along with Simeon and William Reno.[36]

The final passage in the history of the Reno gang occurred about a month later in the latter part of November 1868, when one day a passenger car was dropped off at Seymour, Indiana, some distance from the station. There was nothing remarkable in this, nor did the car attract any attention. That night a train passing through Seymour took up the car and drew it away. A few people about the station when the car was taken up remembered afterwards that this car was filled with strange-looking men who wore Scotch caps and black cloth masks and seemed to be under the command of a tall, dark-haired man addressed by everyone as "Number One." Although there were at least fifty of these men, the conductor of the train could remember nothing about the incident, declaring that he did not enter the car and knew nothing of it being attached to his train. The company of masked men did every-thing in its power to avoid attention, scarcely speaking to each other during the ride and making all movements as noiseless as possible.[37]

The train reached New Albany at two o'clock in the morning. The car was detached and emptied of its fifty men as silently and myste-riously as it had been filled. A few hurried commands were given by "Number One," and then the company marched in quiet order to the jail. Once they arrived, they summoned the jailer to open the doors, but were met with a firm refusal and the shining barrel of a revolver. There followed an exchange of shots, in which the sheriff received a ball in the arm and two local police officers were captured. The jail doors were eventually knocked down; the company entered, and the Reno brothers and their friend, Charlie Anderson, were taken from their cells. Nooses were placed around the men's necks, and the ropes were then looped around the rafters in the corridor of the jail. The outlaws were quickly hanged. The vigilance group then left the building, making sure to lock the doors of the jail behind them. They made their way silently back to the New Albany station, reaching there in time to catch the train that drew out at 3:30 a.m. The special car in which they had come was coupled to this train and dropped off at the switch when Seymour was reached. This was just before daybreak on a dreary November morning.[38]

Who these fifty men were was never discovered, although, because of the fact that Reno and Anderson had been extradited from Great Britain, the general government made an investigation. It was rumored, and generally understood, that the company included some of the most prominent people in Seymour, along with a number of railroad and express employees. It was found that at the time of the lynching, all the telegraph wires leading from New Albany had been cut so that it was noon of the following day before the country learned what had happened.[39]

The newspapers described the leader of the party as a man of unusual stature who wore a handsome diamond ring on the little finger of his right hand. Later some significance was attached to the fact that a well-known railroad official—who answered this description as to stature and had always worn a handsome diamond ring previous to the lynching—ceased to wear his ring for several years afterward.[40]

In February 1878, John Reno was released from prison after serving fifteen years in the Missouri Penitentiary. He returned to Seymour, but by then all of his criminal brothers were dead. In 1885 he was sentenced to three years in the Indiana State Prison for passing counterfeit bills. He died in his home in Seymour on January 31, 1895.[41]

After the agency's "war" with the Renos, the Pinkertons were retained to solve three major bank robberies: the National Village Bank of Bowdoinham, Massachusetts; the Beneficial Savings Fund of America, Philadelphia; and the Walpole, New Hampshire, Savings Bank. Operatives trailed and captured the bank robbers and returned most of the stolen money. In Bowdoinham $80,000 was taken; the vaults of the Philadelphia bank yielded over $1,000,000 in cash and securities; and the New Hampshire bank, $40,000.[42]

MANAGEMENT PRINCIPLES LEARNED FROM THE POSSE AFTER TOM BELL

SURROUND YOURSELF WITH TENS.

Deputy Sheriff Bob Paul of Calaveras County recruited the finest six-gun and rifle shots and trackers in the region to be a part of the posses that tracked down Tom Bell. He found experts in areas that were needed to get the job done and didn't feel threatened by them.

WALK IN SOMEONE ELSE'S SHOES.

Various members of the posses disguised themselves as outlaws and saloon patrons in order to collect the information needed to apprehend the criminals. Instead of figuratively walking in someone else's shoes, posse members made it experiential. By doing this they were in a better position to propose solutions to potential problems and learned how to best achieve their objective.

LEARN TO GIVE UP TRYING TO CONTROL EVERYTHING.

The leaders of the three posses after Tom Bell were comfortable with letting the men riding with them take on extra responsibility. They recognized that being good at their job meant listening to those around them. Officer George Walker listened to posse members, detectives Robert Harrison and Daniel Gay, after they captured one of Bell's gang members. They wanted to persuade the desperado to act as a mole to help guide the other outlaws into a trap.

READ EVERYTHING YOU CAN ABOUT YOUR BUSINESS.

Captain William King pored over newspapers to find out what the press was reporting about the posses' progress. While reading one of the area newspapers, he happened upon a note written to him from the outlaw. The fugitive's rant against the lawman paved the way for one of the posses to ferret the bandit out of hiding.

WAIT. PATIENCE INCREASES YOUR CAPACITY FOR SUCCESS.

A hard-earned discipline for every man with the posses after Tom Bell was patience. Officer Robert Price exercised patience while scanning the banks of the San Joaquin River, and the result was spotting the outlaw as he was trying to find a spot to cross the water. If the lawman had allowed himself to be pressured into generating results, he would have missed seeing the bandit outright.

CHAPTER TWO

SURROUND YOURSELF WITH THE BEST: THE POSSES AFTER TOM BELL

A pair of tired, dust-covered detectives escorted outlaw Tom Bell to a noose dangling off the limb of a sycamore tree. No one spoke a word as the rope was slipped around his thick neck. More than fifteen lawmen from Sacramento, Marysville, and Nevada City, California, made up the posse that apprehended Bell at his hideout at Firebaugh's Ferry near the San Joaquin River. The ruthless highwayman and his gang had eluded the law for more than a year. Bell's reign of terror would end here—a mere four hours after he was captured on Saturday, October 4, 1856.[1]

Bell held in his hand a pair of letters his executioners allowed him to write before they administered justice. Outside of the firm grip he had on his correspondence, he didn't show the least bit of fear. Judge Joseph Belt, the self-appointed hangman and head of the posse, sauntered over to Bell and looked him in the eye. "Do you have anything to say for yourself?" he asked.[2]

"I have no revelations to make," Bell replied. "I would be grateful, however," he added, "to drink to the health of this party present and hope that no personal prejudice has induced them to execute me." Judge Belt nodded to one of his men, who stepped forward with a bottle of whiskey and offered it to Bell.[3]

Bell lifted the bottle to the men and thanked them for their thoughtfulness. "I have no bitterness toward any one of you," he said. He took a drink and handed the bottle back to the lawman. "If you let me now . . . before I go, I'd like to read aloud the letter I wrote to my mother." Judge Belt scanned the faces of his men; no one seemed to have any objections.

"Go on," Belt told the bandit.

Tom unfolded one of the letters in his hand and began reading.[4]

"Dear Mother, I am about to make my exit to another country. I take this opportunity to write you a few lines. Probably you may never hear from me again. If not, I hope we may meet where parting is no prodigal career in the country. I have always recollected your fond admonitions, and if I had lived up to them I would not have been in my present position; but dear Mother, though my fate has been a cruel one, yet I have no one to blame but myself.

"Give my respects to all old and youthful friends. Tell them to beware of bad associations, and never to enter into any gambling saloons, for that has been my ruin. If my old grandmother is living, remember me to her. With these remarks, I bid you farewell forever. Your only boy, Tom."[5]

Bell refolded his letter and bowed his head in prayer. Two lawmen stepped forward, took the letters from him, and tied his hands behind his back. Tom lifted his head and nodded to Judge Belt. His horse was whipped from under him, and he swung into space. Judge Belt's posse was one of three notable posses assembled between March 1856 and October 1856 to track down Tom Bell and his gang of highwaymen that had been terrorizing settlers in the Gold Country.[6]

Tom's trouble with the law began five years prior to being hanged. He hadn't started out to be a thief and a murderer. He was an educated man, and his parents had expected great things from their only

COURTESY OF THE CALIFORNIA HISTORY ROOM, CALIFORNIA STATE LIBRARY, SACRAMENTO, CALIFORNIA

John Craig Boggs was just one of the lawmen chosen to be a part of three notable posses that set out to apprehend Tom Bell.

son. Thomas J. Hodges, later to be known as Tom Bell, was born in Alabama in 1826 and raised in Rome, Tennessee. His mother and father were respected citizens in the community and made sure that Thomas had every advantage, including his schooling. He had the finest teachers who nurtured his natural aptitude for science, and as he got older, he pursued studies in medicine, eventually becoming an accomplished surgeon. After graduating from medical school, Thomas joined the US Army and fought in the Mexican-American War. He served honorably as a noncommissioned officer and was an expert with a rifle and bayonet.[7]

Thomas stood over six feet tall and had blue eyes and sandy hair, with a blond mustache and goatee. His most distinguished physical characteristic was his nose. The once shapely and classic feature had been broken at the bridge and laid flat against his face.[8]

Apart from his unforgettable appearance, he had a personal magnetism and natural leadership qualities. People from all walks of life were drawn to him. Friends and colleagues believed he would be successful in any field of endeavor.[9]

Swept away by the gold-crazy exuberance of the day, Thomas chose to abandon any thought of a medical career or the military in favor of going west. He hoped to strike it rich in California—not as a prospector, but a gambler. The character of most of the people he attracted at saloons and dance halls was dubious, and in time Thomas fell into the evil ways of his associates. He was arrested in October 1851 in Sacramento for grand larceny. He was tried, convicted, and sentenced to five years in prison. The facility where Tom was housed was a brig anchored in San Francisco Bay. When he was being processed into jail, he told the intake guard his name was Tom Bell. Bell was the name of a little-known cattle thief he'd made the acquaintance of in the Stockton area.[10]

The educated outlaw was in jail for five months before he found a way to use his background in medicine to his advantage. The facility did not have a doctor on the premises, and after learning that seriously ill inmates were sent off the brig for treatment, Bell decided to fake an ailment. His experience and knowledge of the workings of the human body helped to make the act convincing. The warden at Angel Island sent Tom to the newly constructed jail called San Quentin for treatment. The novice physician there diagnosed Bell's symptoms as serious and prescribed a regimen of exercises and extended liberties for him.

It was precisely what the highwayman had hoped for, and he used the opportunity to escape.[11]

Bell wasn't alone when he broke out of jail: outlaws Bill Gristy, also known as Bill White; Ned Connor, also known as Ned Covery; and Jim Smith accompanied the doctor. The four escaped convicts formed the nucleus of what would become one of the most notorious gangs in California. Within a month, Tom Bell's band of outlaws consisted of more than thirty men. The choice renegades who rode with Bell yielded to his superior intellect and ability and kept state officials in a fever of excitement for nearly two years.[12]

The desperadoes rendezvoused at a hideout in the foothills near Auburn. Bell methodically planned their crimes from there, dispatching groups of men to carry out various holdups in Yuba, Placer, and Nevada counties. During the spring and summer of 1856, scarcely a night passed without some lonely traveler, owner of a mercantile or a saloon, or cattle rancher being forced to stare into the muzzle of a persuasive revolver while being relieved of his money or livestock.[13]

Tom and his band of notorious outlaws—which included such men as George Skinner, Adolph Newton, Bob Carr (aka English Bob), Monte Jack, Juan Fernandez, Nicanor Rodriguez, Texas Jack, and Charlie Hamilton—spent a great deal of time at a stage stop known as the California House. Located twenty-five miles from Marysville, the popular establishment was owned and operated by a Madam Cole. The madam had befriended the bandits, not only giving them food and lodging from time to time, but letting them know of the type of freight transported between the California House to another Gold Rush town called Camptonville. With her assistance, the gang successfully stole more than $25,000 in a five-month period. In August 1856, Madam Cole made Tom Bell and his gang aware that a stage containing more than $100,000 would be traveling through the area.[14]

COURTESY OF THE CALIFORNIA HISTORY ROOM, CALIFORNIA STATE LIBRARY, SACRAMENTO, CALIFORNIA

Governor J. Neely Johnson would not authorize a posse to pursue Tom Bell, stating that he needed a special act of the legislature to do so. His inaction prompted some law enforcement agents to take matters into their own hands.

The Langston Express stage was on its way to Dry Creek from Marysville when Bell and five of his gang members intercepted the shipment and demanded the driver throw down his weapon and surrender the cargo to them. The messenger on the stage refused to do as he was told. Grabbing his shotgun, he proceeded to fire on the robbers. The gang returned fire, killing Mrs. Tilghman, the wife of a Marysville barber, and wounding three other passengers, all inside the stage. The

Bell gang was uninjured in the exchange of gunfire and escaped without the money.[15]

Tom and his group fled to a hotel and tavern called the Mountaineer House, run by John Phillips. Phillips had come to the country from Australia, where he was a convict from a penal colony. Like Madam Cole, he enjoyed the company of Tom Bell and the gang and let them know which patrons were carrying large sums of money. Phillips received a cut of the funds that the Bell gang stole from the unsuspecting patrons.[16]

On March 12, 1856, Phillips had provided information to Bell about a prospector who had a considerable amount of money in his wallet. The miner was traveling with four other men on a mule train transporting gold to the bank in Sacramento. Bell and his band stopped the train in a densely wooded stretch of trees on the Auburn Road. Riding with the five miners, a Wells Fargo guard named S. T. Barstow attempted to keep the Bell gang at bay by reaching fast for his rifle. Tom beat him to the draw but didn't shoot him.[17]

"Stop that," Tom warned the guard. "We don't want to kill you, but we must have your money." Realizing he was outnumbered and outgunned, the guard tossed his weapon aside and threw up his hands. Bell's gang members tied the men to trees and then stole $21,000 in gold. Similar robberies took place again and again. Bell preferred that no blood be shed when the thefts were taking place but wasn't afraid to kill anyone who tried to interfere with the process.[18]

Bell and his men became rich in a short time. Foothill residents and business owners tired of being victimized wanted Bell and his men stopped. Vigilantes and lone, daring law enforcement agents hunted the gang throughout Northern California without success. Posters describing the fugitives were circulated and rewards offered. Newspapers ran scathing editorials about the inadequacies of law enforcement and challenged the government to organize a ranger company to bring in Bell.[19]

"What is the result of this failure to catch one who is, after all, only an ordinary man?" inquired the editor of the *Sacramento Union*. "It is incumbent upon our state authorities to take immediate steps in the premises."[20]

California governor J. Neely Johnson responded in writing to the remarks, noting that the state had "no arms at its disposal, no power to authorize the fitting out and maintaining of such a company," and that "a special act of legislature was necessary before a state-mandated posse could be assembled."[21]

Some law enforcement agents refused to wait for a special act of legislature to form a posse. Deputy Sheriff Bob Paul of Calaveras County put together the first of three heedless posses to go after Tom Bell and his boys. Deputy Sheriff Paul suspected Jack Phillips of harboring criminals at the Mountaineer House and believed that some of those criminals were part of Tom Bell's gang. The deputy sheriff recruited some of the finest shots and trackers in the region to help him get close enough to the roadhouse to take a look around.[22]

Deputy Sheriff Paul, Undersheriff B. F. Moore, and three others surrounded the tavern and watched the comings and goings of various patrons. Late one evening, Deputy Sheriff Paul disguised himself as an outlaw and entered the saloon. While working undercover, the lawman was able to collect enough damning evidence against the owner of the establishment to place him under arrest. On September 29, 1856, Jack Phillips was taken into custody for suspicion of harboring Tom Bell himself. Three other men were arrested along with Jack Phillips—John Gardner and two brothers with the last name of Farnsworth. All three were members of Tom Bell's gang. Tom was nowhere to be found, but some of his belongings were discovered at the establishment.[23]

On September 30, 1856, William Henson, sheriff of Placer County and head of one of the three notable posses formed to apprehend Tom

Bell, received word from Charley Hamilton, a member of Bell's gang, that Tom and two other outlaws with him had just been seen crossing the Folsom Bridge and were settling in the town of Folsom for the evening. Hamilton, a runaway slave from South Carolina, made a deal with Sheriff Henson that if he supplied information about the bandits' whereabouts, he would be given his freedom.[24]

Sheriff Henson and the other posse members he had picked—deputies John C. Boggs, George Martin, Sam Barrett, and Dana Perkins, all expert rifle shots—hurried to the rendezvous spot. Charley sat at the southeast corner of Jack Phillips's Mountaineer House, waiting for them. The lawmen were a mile from the tavern when they heard the sound of horses fast approaching. It was Hamilton riding to meet the men and guide them to the place where Bell was staying. Boggs and Hamilton rode in advance of the other posse members toward the hotel where Bell was holed up, called the Franklin House. A group of riders passed them coming from the hotel, and, as they neared Hamilton, he recognized them as Tom Bell and his gang. Hamilton told Boggs who the riders were, and Boggs shouted after the men to give themselves up. Bell had no intention of doing so. He spurred his ride forward, not knowing he was now caught between the posse members.[25]

Flashes of gunfire and clouds of gun smoke quickly filled the air. The gun battle didn't last long. One of the lawmen's horses was wounded, and Bell's good friend, Ned Conway, was killed at the scene. Bell himself and another gang member made a complete getaway and disappeared into the night.[26]

Tom Bell and the bandits with whom he traveled were not wounded in the exchange of gunfire with Sheriff Henson's posse, and they hurried on to another favorite resort, the Western Exchange on the Nevada–Sacramento road. The public house was kept by Mrs. Elizabeth Hood, alias Mrs. Cullers, and her three daughters. Bell wanted time to regroup and assess his situation before deciding what to do next. He also wanted a chance to taunt certain law enforcement agents he had read were pursuing him. A Marysville police officer, Captain William King, had been called by the local community to organize an unofficial search for the gang. Tom penned a letter to Captain King and had it sent to the *Marysville Express*. The note of defiance appeared in the September 30, 1856, edition of the paper:

"Don't think for a moment that your vigilance causes me any uneasiness, or that I seek for an armistice," Bell's note read. "No, far from it, for I have unfurled my banner to the breeze, and my motto is 'Catch me if you can!' Captain, I know you are pretty smart, but I think if you would only travel with me a short time I would teach you some tricks that you have never thought of. Probably, you hear a great many things, but must know I am not guilty of every accusation that is alleged against me. For instance, some malicious scoundrel tried to saddle the murder at Frenchman's Bar on me, but he could not do it, and although I am looked upon as a desperado and know I could expect no lenience at the hands of the people should they catch me, still I am too proud to commit such an atrocious and cowardly murder as that was. Truly yours, Tom Bell."[27]

While Bell was contemplating his next move at the Western Exchange, a portion of his band—known as the Walker branch, with its headquarters in Folsom—was engaged in their own drama. George Walker was the leader of Bell's Folsom group, and working alongside him were desperadoes Chip Walker, Bill Gristy, Adolph Newton, Nick Anora, William Carter, and Domingo. They had robbed Wells Fargo Company's express of $26,000 on Scott's Mountain in Shasta County and buried the money. George Walker had Domingo shot for wanting to return and procure the buried treasure. Detectives Robert Harrison and Daniel C. Gay were detailed from the Sacramento force to capture or destroy this band. Yuba County detective Jim Anderson also joined

Camptonville, California, was one of the Gold Rush towns where valuable freight was loaded, and later stolen, by desperado Tom Bell.

the cause, accompanied by two others: former Union soldier A. J. Barclay and a Marysville butcher who was as good with a gun as he was a meat cleaver. They captured one of Bell's gang members, a man named Woodruff, alias Tom Brown, whom they induced to betray the others. He was so long in making up the case that Gay abandoned it and went east. Finally they found Walker, Anora, Gristy, and Newton at Folsom and laid down their plans for capturing them. Newton was caught while alone, sent to Sacramento, and placed on board the "prison brig."[28]

The party, then consisting of Brown, Harrison, J. M. Anderson (marshal of Marysville), and Captain A. J. Barclay and the butcher, both from Marysville, proceeded cautiously to the tent where the out-laws were staying. Anderson and Harrison each had a double-barreled shotgun loaded with buckshot. The plan was for Brown to throw open the tent door while Harrison and Anderson sprang inside and cov-ered the inmates with their guns; if a shot was fired, then those outside were to riddle the tent with bullets. The plan was executed, and the two men sprang in and demanded an instant surrender. Lying on the table were several six-shooters, cocked; Walker, who stood in front of the table arranging his necktie, cried, "No, never!" and seized one of them as quick as a flash and fired, the ball passing between the heads of the two officers. The two men and those outside then fired, and Walker fell dead with a charge of buckshot through his heart. Gristy lifted up the canvas of the tent and crawled out, at the same time continuously firing his revolver over his shoulder. A charge of buckshot fired after his van-ishing figure inflicted only a severe scalp wound. Anora attempted to crawl through the same hole, but was wounded and captured.[29]

Others in the band were killed or captured in various places; the whole region was in arms, and Bell realized that the place was get-ting uncomfortably warm. He managed, by threats and persuasions, to induce Mrs. Hood to remove to the Four Creeks country near the Mer-ced River. Bell then stole a horse and headed south to Firebaugh's Ferry near the San Joaquin River.[30]

An officer named Robert Price, who was part of the third posse of importance, spotted Tom Bell fording the San Joaquin. He was riding away from Firebaugh's Ferry and then stopped to talk to three other riders. Robert quickly urged his horse into a gallop and raced to the camp where Judge Belt and eight members of his posse were wait-ing. Before becoming the first judge of Stockton, California, Belt was a forty-niner, businessman, and Confederate sympathizer who organized the Mason Henry Gang in California during the Civil War. The men he selected as his posse were Southern sympathizers with a talent for hunting and shooting.[31]

Why Tom didn't hear the approaching hoofbeats is a mystery. Perhaps he was just absorbed in a deep conversation with the three riders he met, or maybe he assumed that Robert Price and the other men were hunters pursuing an elk. The judge instantly recognized Bell by his flattened nose and wasted no time drawing his weapon on the outlaw. Bell was taken completely by surprise. Judge Belt ordered the men to throw up their hands and drop their weapons.[32]

"Get the ropes, boys," Belt directed.[33]

While he kept his weapon leveled at the men, Price and the other posse members bound their prisoners' hands behind them after relieving them of additional guns and knives.[34]

Then, while the judge started off on horseback, his companions followed on foot, leading their prisoners over a long, dusty trail until they met the other members of the posse and proceeded with them back to Firebaugh's Ferry.[35]

Reaching the town, one of the posse members suggested that Sheriff Mulford be sent for, but the proposal met with vigorous opposition. Obviously the possemen, recalling those who had been killed and wounded by Bell's gang, were not in the mood for legal proceedings and insisted that the bandits should pay the penalty without delay.[36]

Hearing that, Bell said that he was ready to die, but would ask one last favor—the privilege of writing two farewell letters, one to his mother and the other to a friend. The request was granted, and Bell was led to a vacant cabin. There, surrounded by eager executioners, he sat down with paper and pencil. The friend Tom wrote a letter to was Elizabeth Hood, owner and operator of the Western Exchange.[37]

"Mrs. Hood, my dear and only friend now in this country," Bell's letter began. "As I am not allowed the liberty of seeing you," the correspondence continued, "I have been given the privilege of writing you a few lines, as I have but a few moments to live. I am at a great loss for something to say. I have been fully betrayed. I am accused of every robbery that has been committed for the past twelve months, which is entirely false. I have never committed but three highway robberies in my life; but still I am to blame and my fate is sealed. I am to die like a dog, and there is but one thing that grieves me, and that is the condition of you and your family. Probably I have been instrumental for your misfortunes.

"In my last moments I will think of the many favors you have done for me, and if I had fifty kingdoms to present, you should have them all. But alas! I am poor and my fate is sealed. I would like to give you some advice, but fear you may think me presumptuous. What I would say is this: That you had better send the girls to San Francisco to the Sisters of Charity. There they will be educated and taken care of. Tell all the girls farewell! Tell them to be good girls and to be very careful to whom they pledge themselves for life. All the money I have is ten dollars to be given to Mr. Chism for Sarah. If you see Edward S., tell him my fate. Good-bye forever, Thomas J. Bell."[38]

According to the October 24, 1856, edition of the *Sonoma County Journal*, Mrs. Hood knew Tom Bell as George Brooks. It's how he introduced himself to her and her daughters when they first met, and he never revealed who he actually was until the note he wrote to Elizabeth just before his execution. At one time Tom wanted Elizabeth to live on a ranch in the Four Creeks area near Visalia, California, and go into the business of raising cattle, using the livestock he had stolen from various ranches in and around Placer and Yuba counties. Elizabeth would never consent to the move. She did occasionally visit Bell's gang at their headquarters in a secluded cave in the Sierra Mountains. She recalled that it was difficult to get to and access because the massive boulders surrounding the hideout and lining the rugged trail to the cave allowed enough room for only one or two people at a time.[39]

More than a week after Bell was hanged, an ad appeared in the October 17, 1856, edition of the *Sonoma County Journal* inviting the owners of the cattle stolen by the outlaw to claim their property near Judge Belt's ranch. Any livestock not claimed was to be sold at auction and the money divided between members of the three main posses that had tracked Bell. The funds were to serve as reimbursement for their efforts.[40]

Articles about the hanging of Tom Bell appeared in newspapers across the country. Some reported that his crimes rivaled those of the Mexican bandit Joaquin Murrieta, and others praised the "brave men who rode with the posses to find and stop the fiend Tom Bell and his gang."[41]

A story in the October 5, 1856, edition of the *San Francisco Call* noted that "the fate of the desperado in California is becoming a certain one. Let Tom Bell's fate be a warning to all who today are treading in the path which led him to the gallows."[42]

Bell was twenty-six when the posse led by Judge Belt overtook the outlaw and made him pay with his life for the crimes he had committed.[43]

MANAGEMENT PRINCIPLES LEARNED FROM THE POSSE AFTER THE DOOLIN–DALTON GANG

DIVIDE AND CONQUER.

Posse leaders after the first outlaw gang to rob a train determined early on that the best way to capture the bandits was to employ an age-old plan of attack. Deputy US Marshal John Hixon decided to gain an advantage over the desperadoes by dividing the posse in two. The lawmen were able to overtake several of the bandits in Ingalls, Oklahoma.

INSPIRE TRUST.

The first job of a leader is to inspire trust. Deputy US Marshal Bill Tilghman inspired trust in politicians and law enforcement agents throughout the Oklahoma Territory. Lawman Bat Masterson called him the "best of us all." It was only natural that Tilghman would be called on to help capture the Doolin–Dalton Gang. Tilghman knew trust was the single most essential element to the ability to deliver extraordinary results in an enduring way. To assist him in tracking the notorious train robbers, Tilghman called on two men he trusted with his life: Heck Thomas and Chris Madsen. These men became legendary in their pursuit of outlaws.

BE STEADFAST AND RELENTLESS.

Marshal Tilghman and his posse were driven to succeed. The Doolin–Dalton Gang eluded them for a while, but the lawmen were single-minded in their pursuit. Action combined with commitment results in success. In the case of the Doolin–Dalton Gang, it resulted in the deaths of criminals.

KNOW WHEN TO IGNORE PUBLIC PERCEPTION.

The Doolin–Dalton Gang's reputation for being able to evade the law was well documented, and many doubted the outlaws would ever be apprehended. If the posse after the gang had believed that theirs was a "futile endeavor," as the newspapers described it, the lawmen never would have begun the search for them. The posse never entertained the idea that tracking the lawbreakers was folly, because in their minds, there was no other option beyond getting the bad guys. If the path the posse followed wasn't successful, it didn't mean it was time to give up; it just meant that it was time to shift tactics.

BE WILLING TO ACCEPT ADVICE.

Bill Doolin had been hiding out in New Mexico for weeks, and the posse after the outlaw was unable to locate him. One of the posse members reminded officer Heck Thomas that Doolin was hopelessly in love with his wife and adored his child and would eventually come out of hiding to try and get to his family. It was suggested that the posse travel to Oklahoma where Doolin's wife lived and wait for the desperado to appear. The advice paid off. Doolin did return home, where the posse was waiting for him.

CHAPTER THREE

BE STEADFAST AND RELENTLESS: THE POSSE AFTER THE DOOLIN-DALTON GANG

One of the grisliest battles between outlaws and lawmen took place on September 3, 1893, twelve miles east of Stillwater, Oklahoma, at the town of Ingalls. More than ten people who were situated on the eastern edge of Payne County only a few miles from the rocky retreats and nearly inaccessible wooded areas of Creek County were killed. For some time it had been the spot where a gang of bandits, murderers, train robbers, and horse thieves, known as the Doolin–Dalton Gang, had made their headquarters.[1]

The 250 people who resided in Ingalls had decided it was better business and safer to accept the outlaws who had overtaken the town than to fight them. In return for not robbing local merchants, outlaws could get drunk in an Ingalls saloon without having to shoot their way out, and they could rent a bed in Mary Pierce's hotel (with or without a girl in it) and not have to worry about waking up with a sheriff's gun in their chests.[2]

The members of the Doolin–Dalton Gang were the last great bandits of the Old West. Bill Doolin and William Dalton worked together at the H-X Bar Ranch in Oklahoma Territory. In 1891, they decided life as ranch hands was too sedate and traded in their legitimate jobs to rob trains and banks. Federal marshals began pursuing the gang in October 1892, after the daring outlaws attempted a double-band holdup in Coffeyville, Kansas. The gang was comprised of more than eight men. In addition to the Dalton boys and Bill Doolin, there were also George Newcomb (alias Bitter Creek), Tom Jones (aka Roy Daugherty), William "Texas Jack" Blake, and Dan Clifton (alias Dynamite Dick).[3]

It wasn't until after the Doolin–Dalton Gang held up two trains in the Cherokee Outlet at Wharton in Oklahoma that law enforcement learned the outlaws were hiding in caves outside Ingalls, Oklahoma, and as an extension, Ingalls itself. Deputy US Marshal John Hixon rode toward Ingalls on Thursday, August 31, 1892. Among the fourteen members of the posse with him were marshals L. J. Shadley, T. J. Houston, Dick Speed, and Jim Masterson. They had received information that the gang was rendezvousing at the hotel at nine in the morning. The posse decided to separate and make their way into Ingalls from different directions. They would surround the town and move in to capture the outlaws on Friday, September 1, 1892.[4]

The Pierce Hotel was a two-story structure that possessed an almost unobstructed view of the entire town. A woman named Anderson, commonly reported to be George Newcomb's girlfriend, was at the hotel when the posse began approaching Ingalls from the north, northwest, and northeast. While on the balcony surveying the sights, Newcomb's paramour saw something suspicious moving in the middle distance. Other gang sympathizers noticed the activity, too, and reported to Bill Doolin. An alarm warning the outlaws that the law was closing in sounded throughout the burg.[5]

Four of the five bandits hurried across the street to Ransom's Saloon, where a fifth bandit was waiting, and prepared to open fire on the fast-approaching posse. Tom Jones stayed behind at the hotel in an upstairs room, ready to cover his colleagues when and if they retreated.

Deputy US Marshal Heck Thomas.

US marshals and deputy marshals in Paris, Texas. Heck Thomas is seated second from right; Chris Madsen is seated directly behind Heck.

Tom had no sooner loaded his gun and aimed out the window than the lawmen opened fire on the outlaws in the saloon. The desperadoes returned fire. Bullets pierced buildings and shattered glass.[6]

Dallas Simmons, a young man of about twenty-three years old and an innocent bystander, was one of the first victims to be killed. He fell mortally wounded after having been shot through the hips and bowels. Immediately afterward, Dick Speed was shot through the stomach and died of his wounds. Owen Walker, a businessman from out of town, fell, too—killed by a bullet to the liver. T. J. Houston was then shot in the left thigh and the lower abdomen. He would die the following day. L. J. Shadley was also killed after being shot three times in the chest.[7]

The lawmen left standing kept up a regular fusillade on Ransom's Saloon until after twelve o'clock. At that time, the four bandits in the saloon made their way to the adjoining livery stable, where their horses were quartered, saddled them up, and rode away toward the southwest. As they departed, a heavy firing was kept up by the posse members, resulting in the killing of one of their horses, the severe wounding of another, and the probable wounding of two of the bandits. The five bandits rode away on four horses.[8]

After the escape of the five, full attention was directed to the bandit concealed in the hotel. The fatalities already suffered made the officers cautious, and it was determined that they would burn the building down unless the bandit gave himself up. By three in the afternoon, Tom Jones had surrendered.[9]

The posse determined that Jones had shot and killed more people than anyone else. Concealed in the hotel, he had a complete survey of the entire town, and, every time a man exposed himself, he would pick him off. Jones had killed Dick Speed, Dallas Simmons, T. J. Houston, and L. J. Shadley.[10]

Of the outlaws, the posse determined that Bill Doolin had a broken arm; Bill Dalton was wounded two or three times about the stomach; and George Newcomb was wounded in the left groin.[11]

Seven or eight horses and mules were killed during the melee. It was estimated that at least five hundred shots were exchanged. Ransom's Saloon was riddled with bullets, and the portion of the town where the conflict occurred looked like a battle scene from a war.[12]

As soon as the news of the trouble in Ingalls reached Stillwater, Oklahoma, Sheriff F. M. Burdick organized a posse to set out after the Doolin–Dalton Gang. Payne County attorney S. P. King and Deputy Freeman E. Miller, both proficient at shooting, joined the search. King was armed with warrants to arrest the outlaws for robbing banks in

Bentonville, Arkansas, and in western Kansas and for some train robberies on the Santa Fe Railroad. The bandits were last seen heading in the direction of Cushing.[13]

While Sheriff Burdick was leading his posse toward Cushing, US Marshal Evett Nix summoned Deputy US Marshal Bill Tilghman to his office to discuss the ongoing problems with the Doolin–Dalton Gang. Nix had received numerous complaints about the outlaws, and they wanted the matter resolved, even if it meant additional posses had to be formed to find the desperadoes. Tilghman believed he could get the job done with a few good men and selected two to join him in the search: deputy US marshals Heck Thomas and Chris Madsen.[14]

Heck Thomas's background in law enforcement was extensive. In 1865, he had joined the Atlanta police force and gained fame as a fearless fighter after being wounded in one of the city's race riots. In 1875, he hired on as a guard for the Texas Express Company. He was promoted to detective in 1876 after preventing a train robbery by hiding money in an unlit stove. As a detective, he led posses that captured several members of the Sam Bass Gang. Thomas turned to bounty hunting in 1885, capturing two outlaw brothers, Jim and Pink Lee.[15]

Thomas was appointed a deputy US marshal later that year and moved to Fort Smith, Arkansas. Under the jurisdiction of "Hanging Judge" Isaac Parker, Thomas pursued outlaws and fugitives in the Indian Territory.[16]

Denmark-born Chris Madsen came to the United States in 1876 to fight Indians and held the post of Oklahoma Territory marshal for twenty-five years. He was responsible for the capture of numerous fugitives and was a well-respected lawman. In 1891, Madsen became a deputy US marshal and is credited with apprehending or killing more than one hundred outlaws.[17]

Tilghman chose Thomas and Madsen to assist him in the pursuit of the Doolin–Dalton Gang because they were tenacious, courageous, and devoted friends he knew he could trust and count on. After swapping information about the gang, the trio decided the first thing they needed to do was ride the frontier from Kansas to Texas and visit every ranch and farm to see what they could find out about the outlaw group. The three decided to split up and meet in Guthrie a month later to compare notes.[18]

Tilghman called on the H-X Bar Ranch first. The large spread along the banks of the Cimarron River was owned by wealthy Texas cattleman Oscar Halsell. Halsell confirmed that Bill Doolin did work for him at one time. Doolin was young and eager, and Halsell believed he would be a good hand. He wasn't much for working with livestock, but he was good with an ax and could split rails quickly and efficiently. In the evenings, Doolin pored over books, teaching himself to read and write. Halsell theorized the hired hand had a wild nature, was ambitious, and that it was this combination that prompted him to break the law.[19]

When Tilghman, Thomas, and Madsen met again in Guthrie, they exchanged similar stories about the gang members. Some said they weren't desperadoes because of a "wild nature," but rather that they wanted revenge against a society they felt had treated them poorly. The lawmen concluded the gang was composed of emotionally stunted men, driven by fear and hate.[20]

After the Battle at Ingalls, Tilghman's posse learned that the Doolin–Dalton Gang was headed northeast of the town. The trio of lawmen followed the lead.[21]

On the evening of January 3, 1894, two members of the gang entered the Clarkson, Oklahoma, post office, held up the postmaster, and looted the mail. Two weeks later, Bill Doolin, along with Tulsa Jack and Dynamite Dick, robbed the Farmers Citizens Bank of Pawnee of

Members of the Doolin–Dalton Gang having met their end.

$300; on March 10, the gang robbed the Santa Fe Railroad station at Woodward, Oklahoma, stealing the army payroll of more than $6,500.[22]

Tilghman's posse was steadfast and relentless. They followed the outlaws' trail of criminal activity, sometimes less than a day or so behind their next illegal act. Deputy marshals Steve Burke and Neal Brown had now joined the lawmen. The way the bandits had managed to elude them frustrated the posse. They had determined they were being watched and their movements reported back to the gang leader, but just who the spies were was to remain a mystery for the time being.[23]

News that the gang members had been spotted in the Seminole Nation prompted the posse to hurry to the western part of Oklahoma. By the time they arrived, Bill Dalton and Bitter Creek had robbed a general store and killed a marshal in the process.

The Doolin–Dalton Gang's reputation for being able to evade the law continued to grow. The outlaws' sense of invincibility grew as well. On May 10, 1894, the outlaws robbed a bank in Southwest City, Missouri. The bandits were overconfident about getting away without harm. The citizens in the small Ozark Mountains community decided to fight back against the thieves and opened fire on them as they attempted to make their escape. Before the gunfight ended, a respected member of Southwest City had been killed, but several members of the gang were injured, including Bill Doolin.[24]

The wounded gang quickly fled the area and hid out in the southeastern portion of Missouri. They hoped to heal and regroup before they embarked on another crime spree. Bill Dalton was too despondent over the failed robbery and didn't want to do anything but drink. In his drunken depression, he regretted his life of crime and being upstaged by Bill Doolin. Dalton felt leadership of the unsavory group should have fallen to him and not Doolin. He refused to get sober and participate in any illegal deeds planned by Doolin. Doolin realized how impossible it was to try and reason with a drunkard and decided the gang should split up. Dalton was not happy with the decision and vowed to organize a terrifying group of gangsters that would be loyal to him and steal more money than Doolin ever dreamed of having.[25]

Dalton traveled to Texas to acquire the bandit partners he needed to keep his criminal enterprise moving forward. The first outing with the new gang members was disastrous. The majority of the men Dalton attracted were drunks like himself, and most had been drinking the day they robbed the First National Bank in Longview, Texas, of $2,000. Dalton's gang left a string of dead bodies behind as they rode out of town on May 23, 1894.[26]

Dalton fled to the home of a friend who lived in Ardmore, Oklahoma, and proceeded to drink himself into a stupor. He was unaware that a posse had tracked him to the location. On June 8, 1894, the lawmen surrounded the house and demanded that he surrender. Dalton refused and was subsequently killed. The demise of the notorious criminal was reported in newspapers across the country.[27]

The June 15, 1894, edition of the *King City Chronicle* announced, "The identification is complete. His widow is here under arrest and has sent two telegrams, signing her name 'Mrs. Jennie Dalton.' The first went to C. H. Blivens, 1407 Van Ness Avenue, San Francisco, and read: 'My husband, Bill Dalton, lies here dead. Come at once. I want his remains sent home.' The other one was addressed to Mrs. A. L. Dalton, Kingfisher, and read: 'Bill Dalton here dead. Come at once if you wish to see him.'"[28]

The circumstances surrounding the killing of Dalton were also included in the article announcing his death. "Yesterday while the posse was taking their positions, Dalton was seen to come out, look around, and immediately return," the *King City Chronicle* story explained. "The officers on the east side were discovered by him through a window or by someone in the house, and pistol in hand, he jumped through a window on the north and started to run east. One of the posse members was less than thirty yards from the house and called on him to halt. For reply he tried to take aim while running and just then the Winchester of the officer spoke.

"The two jumps into the air were the only motions after this by the fleeing man. His pistol fell from his hand and with a groan he sank down. Mr. Hart ran up to him and asked what he was doing there, but he was too near dead to reply, and expired without a word. The house was searched, and over 150 letters, besides numerous rolls of crisp bank bills, were found, the address proving him to be Bill Dalton and the money proving him to have been the leader of the Longview Bank robbery.[29]

The bank windows in Coffeyville, Kansas, show a few of the bullet holes fired by citizens and bandits during the robbery in 1892.

"Between $35,000 and $50,000 will be paid by three states, two territories, and the United States authorities to the nine officers who composed the posse when Dalton was killed."[30]

Tilghman and the posse he organized were happy to hear that Bill Dalton's reign of terror was over. Since learning Dalton and Doolin had gone their separate ways, Tilghman and his men had kept their focus on Doolin. Indeed, bringing Doolin down had been a direct order from Marshal Nix.[31]

In late January 1895, after tracking Bill Doolin across five states, Bill Tilghman and Deputy Neal Brown located the outlaw and his band outside Guthrie, Oklahoma. He happened on the outlaw gang early one snowy morning. More than six outlaws were hiding in a dugout, sleeping. Tilghman decided it would be wise to hurry to town and bring reinforcements to the site. By the time the rest of the posse was gathered and had returned to the dugout, the bandits were gone. Thus, the pursuit continued.[32]

Between February and July 1895, Tilghman's posse managed to track and arrest all but three key members of Doolin's gang. By mid-summer only Little Dick West, Dynamite Dick Clifton, and Bill Doolin himself remained at large. During his long search for the elusive outlaws, Tilghman had deduced that two young women had been working with Doolin and filtering information to him about what law enforcement agents were after, and their approximate locations. Tilghman had kept a careful eye out for the females as he rode, and finally, in mid-August 18, 1895, he had them in his sights.[33]

On the afternoon of August 18, 1895, Marshal Tilghman and Deputy Marshal Steve Burke led their horses toward a small farm outside Pawnee, Oklahoma. The lawmen had tracked a pair of outlaws to the location and were proceeding cautiously when several gunshots were fired.[34]

Tilghman caught sight of a Winchester rifle sticking out a broken window of a dilapidated cabin. He spurred his horse out of the line of fire just as the weapon went off. He steered his mount around the building and arrived at the back door the same time sixteen-year-old Jennie Stevens, alias Little Britches, burst out the house. She shot at him with a pistol while racing to a horse waiting nearby.[35]

By the time Tilghman settled his ride and drew his weapon, Jennie was on her horse. She turned the horse away from the cabin, kicked it hard in the ribs, and the animal took off. Tilghman leveled his firearm at the woman and shot. Jennie's horse stumbled and fell, and she was tossed from the animal's back, losing her gun in the process.[36]

The marshal hopped off his own ride and hurried over to the stunned and annoyed runaway. Jennie picked herself up quickly and cursed her misfortune. She charged the lawman, dug her fingernails

Bob and Grat Dalton after the Dalton gang attempted to rob the Coffeyville, Kansas, bank on October 13, 1892.

into his neck, and slapped him several times before he could subdue her. He was a battered man when he finally pinned her arms behind her back.[37]

Back at the cabin, Deputy Marshal Steve Burke wrestled a gun away from thirteen-year-old Annie McDougal, alias Cattle Annie, a rail-thin young woman wearing a gingham dress and a wide-brimmed black straw hat. The pistol she tried to shoot him with was lying in the dirt several feet in front of her.[38]

Two years prior to their apprehension and arrest, Cattle Annie and Little Britches were riding with the Doolin gang, a notorious band of outlaws who robbed trains and banks. Enamored by the fame of the well-known criminals, the teenage girls had decided to leave home and follow the bandits. They helped the criminals steal cattle, horses, guns, and ammunition, and warned them whenever law enforcement was on their trail.[39]

Legend tells that Bill Doolin gave Cattle Annie and Little Britches their nicknames. Cattle Annie was born Anna Emmaline McDougal in Kansas in 1882. Jennie Stevens was born in 1879 in Oklahoma. Both girls had run afoul of the law before joining the Doolin gang. Each sold whiskey to Osage Indians. According to the September 3, 1895, edition of the Ada, Oklahoma, newspaper, the *Evening Times*, Jennie seemed to have "plied her vocation for a long time successfully, going in the guise of a boy tramp hunting work." Between selling liquor to Indians and life with the Doolins, Jennie had married a deaf-mute named MidKiff, and Annie rustled livestock.[40]

News of Cattle Annie and Little Britches's arrest was reported in the August 21, 1895, edition of the Cedar Rapids, Iowa, newspaper, the *Evening Gazette*. "A deputy marshal and a posse arrested two notorious female outlaws but had to fight to make the arrest," the article read. "The marshal's posse ran into them, and they showed fight. Several shots were fired before they gave up. One was in men's clothing."[41]

It wasn't until Cattle Annie and Little Britches had been arrested that Tilghman decided to concentrate on locating Bill Doolin's wife and son. He reasoned that if he found his wife and family, the outlaw might be close by. He searched for weeks before he got a lead that a man meeting Doolin's description with a wife and child was living near Burden, Kansas. Tilghman traveled to the Kansas town and learned that the couple he was looking for was going by the name of Wilson.[42]

Tilghman kept out of sight and watched the Wilsons' cabin for several days. He recognized the woman living there as Doolin's wife, Edith, but Doolin was nowhere around. He checked the mail that came to the home when Edith was out and noticed a letter from Mary Pierce, the woman who owned the hotel in Ingalls where the Doolin–Dalton Gang often stayed. Tilghman opened the letter and learned that Doolin was in Eureka Springs, Arkansas, soaking in the therapeutic waters there as a way of combating his rheumatism. Tilghman planned to ride to Eureka Springs, but the morning he was set to leave, Edith was heading out, too, and Tilghman decided to follow her. She drove a buggy to the railroad depot in Burden where the lawman watched her purchase a ticket to Perry, Oklahoma. He then sent a wire to Marshal Nix to have men posted in Perry to watch for her. Tilghman was moving on to Eureka Springs.[43]

Bill Doolin was getting a shave at a barbershop when Bill Tilghman found him in Eureka Springs on January 12, 1896. The lawman was disguised as an itinerant preacher, and the outlaw didn't pay much attention to him when he entered the business and ordered a bath. "Tilghman went into the bathroom, and, through a crack in the door, watched his man," the January 23, 1896, edition of the *Weekly Republican-Traveler* reported. "The latter soon grew interested in a paper, and

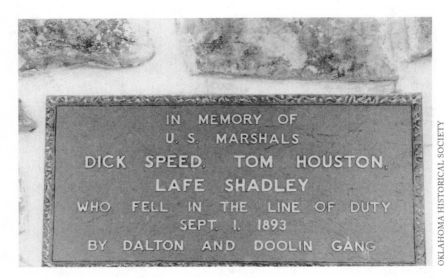

OKLAHOMA HISTORICAL SOCIETY

A plaque in Ingalls, Oklahoma, commemorates the men who lost their lives while pursuing the Doolin–Dalton Gang.

the marshal pulled his revolver, walked up to within four feet of Doolin, covered him, and said, sharply: 'Bill! Throw up your hands!'

"He got his hands halfway up, raised to his feet, looked his captor square in the eye, and seemed to be determining whether to put his hands up or go for his gun. Tilghman said: 'Bill, you know who I am, don't you?' 'Yes, I do,' was the reply. 'Well, then,' said Tilghman, 'you had better get your hands up.' The hands went up, and Bill Doolin was a prisoner.

"Tilghman shackled and handcuffed the captive and informed him they were going to take the train back to Guthrie where Doolin would be tried. At the train Doolin said: 'Tilghman, if you will take off my shackles, I will pledge my word not to try to escape. You know that my word is good. Take off my shackles and you can go to sleep, if you want to go, but you will find me on the train when you wake up. If you know anything at all about me, you know that Bill Doolin's word is good.' Tilghman took off the shackles, called for no help, told Doolin to take a seat in front of him, and came through without any trouble.

"Doolin says that he knew Tilghman as a brave man by reputation, and had it been any other officer he would have pulled his gun and shot. 'I have been tired of this roving life ever since the first three months I took it up,' Doolin confessed to Tilghman. 'I am glad I am caught. I have done nothing and am ready for trial. I have never wronged any man, and they can't prove a thing on me. I was compelled to stay in the brush because my name got connected with some of the train robbers. I knew some of the boys who did the business, but I had no hand in it. I want to get out of this business and live a quiet peaceful life with my wife and child. I have never been a bad man, and I want to live like other people.'

"The reports for some time have been to the effect that Doolin has been trying to make terms with the officers so that he might take a short term and be left alone to a quiet life. For months he has been dodging and hiding, hunted like a wild animal, afraid to sleep for fear of capture, and living at a tension which must have been trying almost beyond human endurance. Small wonder that capture is to him a relief, and that his imprisonment will be a sweet respite to him, even though he goes from the prison doors into a black and miserably disgraceful and degrading end upon the scaffold."[44]

A large crowd of people were waiting at the Guthrie train station when Marshal Tilghman and Bill Doolin arrived. When Doolin stepped out on the open platform, a hissing sound swept through the crowd. Fearing the angry group was more a lynch mob than merely curious onlookers, Doolin hesitated a bit. Tilghman pushed him on through the gathering to a carriage waiting for them. Once they were in the carriage, mounted outriders led the way to the jail. Doolin was locked in a cell, and an armed guard was posted outside the cell door. The federal attorney set to try Doolin was confident of a conviction, but needed plenty of time to prepare his case. On July 5, 1896, weeks before the trial was to start, Bill Doolin escaped.[45]

According to the July 9, 1896, edition of the *Jefferson Gazette*, of Jefferson, Ohio, Doolin broke out of jail with thirteen other prisoners. They overpowered the guards at 9:30 at night, relieved them of their weapons, and placed them in the cells. Heck Thomas was assigned the task of putting together a posse to go after Doolin once more. A $5,000 reward was offered for the rearrest and conviction of the violent outlaw. Chris Madsen and Neal Brown were two of the officers who accompanied Heck on the hunt for Doolin. Marshal Pat Nagle, Charley Colcord, Frank Canton, and Bob Moore were also part of Thomas's posse.[46]

Bill Doolin hurried to New Mexico and hid out at a ranch near Rhodes Pass owned by writer Eugene Manlove Rhodes. Rhodes frequently allowed outlaws to stay at his place with no questions asked. Those desperadoes would eventually find their way into the novels he penned.[47]

Doolin grew restless waiting at the ranch and longed to see his wife and child. Desperate to be united with them, he left the Southwest and headed back to Oklahoma. Edith Doolin and her son were living on her parents' farm in Lawton, Oklahoma. When Heck Thomas and his posse learned of that fact, they made their way to the homestead and waited for Doolin to appear. Given his actions in the past regarding his family, Thomas speculated Doolin would eventually attempt to see them. The posse wasn't disappointed. Doolin made his appearance on August 25, 1896.[48]

Heck Thomas and three of his possemen spotted Doolin walking his horse onto the property at two o'clock in the morning. The bright, full moon lit up the area, making it clear for the lawmen to spot Doolin

ALVIN RUCKER COLLECTION, OKLAHOMA HISTORICAL SOCIETY

The town of Ingalls, Oklahoma, where the Doolin–Dalton Gang made their home.

shuffling along, carrying a Winchester rifle and whistling as though he hadn't a care in the world. When Thomas called out to Doolin and ordered him to drop his weapon, the outlaw pointed his gun in the direction he heard the voice. One of the possemen fired both barrels of his shotgun in Doolin's direction. The bandit dropped to the ground, dead.[49]

"He was at once loaded in a wagon in waiting, and the team of mules was driven furiously toward the city," a report in the August 26, 1896, edition of the *Kansas City Journal* read. "The body lay in the bottom of the wagon, covered by a blanket. The party arrived here just after noon. When the undertaker dressed the body, he found twenty buckshot wounds in the chest, four having entered the heart, and the left arm was shattered by a Winchester ball. He wore the same clothes he had on when he broke jail, but his face was covered with a heavy beard."[50]

Bill Doolin was thirty-six years old when he died.[51]

MANAGEMENT PRINCIPLES LEARNED FROM THE POSSE AFTER JAMES KENEDY

HOLD MEETINGS THAT DON'T WASTE EVERYONE'S TIME.

There's no easier way to get your coworkers to dislike you than to invite them to a pointless, meandering meeting. When Sheriff Masterson assembled all law enforcement agents in Dodge City on October 4, 1878, the discussion about who was going to go after murderer James Kenedy was quick and direct. The outlaw had an eight-hour head start, and time was of the essence.

CREATE A STRATEGIC ROAD MAP.

A well-planned strategic road map is essential for any posse. It not only tells where you are and the quickest way to get to your destination, but it can also shorten the route. You will waste less time than you would if you were trying to figure things out on the fly. Bat Masterson's posse shared information they knew about the criminal they were set to pursue and the path he would most likely follow, and then determined what they needed to do to capture him.

MAKE SURE YOU HAVE ENOUGH TOOLS TO GET THE JOB DONE.

After you've established the vision, focus, and road map, attention quickly shifts to execution. The "most intrepid posse" didn't leave Dodge City without the appropriate weapons and an adequate supply of ammunition. The lawmen believed they could quickly apprehend Kenedy, but they brought with them enough provisions to see them through if the trek took longer than they expected.

BE PREPARED TO WEATHER ANY STORM.

A severe thunderstorm threatened to halt the posse's pursuit of Kenedy. Even though the rain had washed away any tracks they might have hoped to pick up, they refused to let their disappointment cast a shadow on their objective. While waiting for the sky to clear, the lawmen discussed how the weather would hamper the outlaw's ability to get away and considered what he might do next. The posse arrived on the other side of the storm more determined than ever to chase Kenedy down.

FORGE LASTING ALLIANCES.

The time the posse spent together trailing Kenedy and escorting him back to Dodge City to stand trial created a lasting bond between them. Although they would eventually go their separate ways, the lawmen would call on each other in the future to help with similar jobs. Knowing whom to count on to get the work done is crucial when planning bigger tasks.

CHAPTER FOUR

CREATE A STRATEGIC ROAD MAP:
THE POSSE AFTER JAMES KENEDY

Dora Hand was in a deep sleep. Her bare legs were draped across the thick blankets covering her delicate form, and a mass of long, auburn hair stretched over the pillow under her head and dangled off the top of a flimsy mattress. Her breathing was slow and effortless. A framed, graphite-charcoal portrait of an elderly couple hung above the bed on faded, satin-ribbon wallpaper, watching over her slumber.[1]

The air outside the window was still and cold. The distant sound of voices, backslapping laughter, profanity, and a piano's tinny, repetitive melody wafted down Dodge City's main thoroughfare and snuck into the small room where Dora was sleeping.

Dodge was an all-night town. Walkers and loungers kept the streets and saloons busy. Residents learned to sleep through the giggling, growling, and gunplay of the cowboy consumers and their paramours for hire. Dora was accustomed to the nightly frivolity and clatter. Her dreams were seldom disturbed by the commotion.

All at once the hard thud of a pair of bullets charging through the door and wall of the tiny room cut through the routine noises of the cattle town with uneven, gusty violence. The first bullet was halted by the dense plaster partition leading into the bedchamber. The second struck Dora on the right side under her arm.[2] There was no time for her to object to the injury, no moment for her to cry out or recoil in pain. The slug killed her instantly.

In the near distance, a horse squealed, and its galloping hooves echoed off the dusty street and faded away.

A pool of blood poured out of Dora's fatal wound, turning the white sheets she rested on to crimson. A clock sitting on a nightstand next to the lifeless body ticked on steadily and mercilessly. It was 4:15 in the morning on October 4, 1878, and for the moment nothing but the persistent moonlight filtering into the scene through a closed window marked the thirty-four-year-old woman's passing.

Twenty-four hours prior to Dora's being gunned down in her sleep, she had been onstage at the Alhambra Saloon and Gambling House. She was a stunning woman whose wholesome voice and exquisite features had charmed audiences from Abilene to Austin. She regaled love-starved wranglers and roughriders at stage and railroad stops with her heartfelt renditions of the popular ballads "Blessed Be the Ties that Bind" and "Because I Love You So."

Adoring fans referred to her as the "nightingale of the frontier," and admirers continually competed for her attention. More times than not, pistols were used to settle arguments about who would be escorting Dora back to her place at the end of the evening. Local newspapers claimed her talent and beauty "caused more gunfights than any other woman in all the West."[3]

Dora had arrived in Dodge City in June of 1878. Several of the city's residents who knew the songstress was on her way were eagerly anticipating her arrival. Among them was the mayor of Dodge City, James Kelley. Mayor Kelley had made Dora's acquaintance at Camp Supply. He was smitten with her, and the pair became romantically involved shortly after she stepped off the stage in Dodge.[4]

Bill Tilghman. KANSAS STATE HISTORICAL SOCIETY

James "Spike" Kenedy, the handsome, overly indulged son of Texas cattle baron Mifflin Kenedy, was annoyed that Dora was spending time with the mayor. He hoped to make her his own. James was a tall man with a strong build, and he was accustomed to getting his own way. He wore tailor-made clothes and carried himself with confidence, derived mostly from his family's sizable bank account and landholdings. In September 1878, James strutted into the Alhambra Saloon and Gambling House with the intention of proposing to Dora. He hoped they'd marry quickly, and then he would escort her back to the family ranch. It didn't enter his mind that Dora would reject his offer of marriage in favor of a relationship with the mayor. He was furious when she told him, and his hatred of Mayor Kelley and Dora grew from that day forward.[5]

On October 3, 1878, Dora Hand entertained another standing-room-only crowd at the Alhambra. She courteously accepted the enthusiastic applause, thanked the piano player for accompanying her, said good night to the audience, and exited the tavern to retire for the evening. Men, milling around the streets playfully, whistled and called after her as she walked by them. She hurried along undisturbed to Mayor Kelley's and entered the home as though she were expected.

Mayor Kelley was out of town and had invited Dora and her friend Fannie to stay at his place during his absence. The accommodations were infinitely more quiet and private than a hotel's. The performer tiptoed through the house, making sure not to wake Fannie. After slipping into her bedclothes, she crawled under the covers and drifted off to sleep.[6]

The shots that pierced the walls of Kelley's home at 4:15 in the morning rousted Fannie Garretson from her bed shortly after she'd heard them fired. An eerie stillness hung in the air—a quiet that begged her not to trust it. Fannie glanced down at the quilt across the bed and noticed a burn hole in the fabric. She knew it had been made by a bullet. Slipping her finger into the frayed material, she traced the path of the pistol ball to the wall opposite the bed.

Fannie raced out of the house, her eyes wide with terror, screaming. Shaking and hysterical, she sat down in the alleyway between Mayor Kelley's home and a row of saloons that bordered the building in the back. When the law arrived moments later to investigate, they found Fannie Garretson in her nightgown, sobbing and rocking back and forth. Too upset to speak, she merely pointed at the house and shook her head. "Poor Dora," she later told authorities. "She never spoke, but died unconscious. She was so when she was struck and so she died."

A steady beat of boots hurrying along the wooden-plank sidewalks reverberated off the buildings and overhangs lining Dodge City's Front Street. Curious onlookers peered out of the saloons and bathhouses as two familiar characters sprinted past. Lawmen Wyatt Earp and Jim Masterson, Bat Masterson's younger brother, raced in the direction of town from which a series of four gunshots had popped five minutes earlier.[7]

Both men wore the stern, focused look of peace officers accustomed to living in a dangerous and unpredictable cow town. Each had a commanding presence that warded off as many as it attracted. Each wore a badge on his vest. Wyatt was an impressive man with blond hair, a well-groomed mustache, and blue-gray eyes. His slender frame and erect posture made him appear taller than his six feet. Jim was roughly the same height, with dark hair and a thick mustache that covered the stubborn lines around his thin mouth.

As the men neared the back entrance of the Great Western Hotel, they scanned the area carefully, their hands perched over their pistols, ready to draw if necessary. Fannie Garretson was crouching near the back door of Mayor James Kelley's home, sobbing.

As Earp and Masterson approached, her plaintive eyes met theirs, and, before anyone could speak, she pointed a shaking finger at the house. The men quickly noticed that a bullet had splintered the door of the home. They entered Mayor Kelley's place, lifting their six-shooters out of their holsters as they did. A fast inspection of the various rooms of the house led the lawmen to the spot where Dora Hand lay dead.

The lawmen investigated the crime scene and made the rounds, looking for witnesses. It didn't take them long to deduce that Kenedy was the prime suspect. He'd had several run-ins with the law between

KANSAS STATE HISTORICAL SOCIETY

Bat Masterson.

July and October 1878, and he'd been heard threatening to kill the mayor when he had the chance. The Mastersons and Wyatt met up with fellow lawmen Charlie Bassett and Bill Tilghman to search the town for Kenedy. When the suspect got word that the law was looking for him, he jumped on a fast horse and hurried out of Dodge. The lawmen decided that Kenedy had to be hunted down and made to answer for the crime.[8]

Early on the morning of October 4, Sheriff Bat Masterson assembled all law enforcement agents in the city for a meeting to discuss organizing a posse. It was the general consensus of all the lawmen that Kenedy would be traveling fast back to his father's ranch in Texas. Kenedy had an eight-hour head start, and the sheriff knew he would have to assemble the most capable men to be part of a team that could track a fugitive with that kind of a lead. He knew that whoever set out to search for Kenedy had to be experienced trackers and would have to be riders who could stick in their saddles for days at a time.[9]

Having hunted buffalo with Bill Tilghman and Wyatt Earp, Bat Masterson knew they were skilled and resourceful men. "Wyatt Earp is one of the few men I personally knew whom I regarded as absolutely destitute of physical fear," Bat later wrote about the man. Tilghman was steadfast, an exceptional shot with a rifle, and loyal to the spirit of the law. Bat called him "the greatest of us all." The sheriff knew first-hand the strength of character Charlie Bassett possessed as well. He had worked for Charlie when he was named Dodge City's first sheriff. Bassett's formality in manner and his inborn knowledge of how to get along with people earned him the nickname "Senator." He was at his best when under pressure and had no problem approaching out-of-control men in the midst of a gunfight and disarming them.[10]

A number of men had volunteered to join in the hunt for James Kenedy, but Bat knew the top men for the job were those he knew best.

Local politicians agreed with the sheriff's selection and echoed the sentiments of the *Dodge City Times*, which, on October 12, 1878, called City Marshal Charlie Bassett, Assistant Marshal Wyatt Earp, Sheriff Bat Masterson, and Deputy Sheriff Bill Tilghman "as intrepid a posse as ever pulled a trigger."[11]

At two o'clock in the afternoon on October 4, 1878, the posse loaded their sturdy mounts with their bedrolls, food, guns, and a generous supply of ammunition. Townspeople and ranchers watched the four law-men prepare for the journey. They wished the men well and took turns shaking their hands.[12]

The intrepid posse charged along the Old Santa Fe Trail in search of Kenedy. The horse Kenedy was riding was a racehorse he'd recently purchased, and it hadn't been shod. This would make it hard to pick up the trail. Still, they did the best they could and followed the river road until they came to a place called Mulberry Crossing, twenty-seven miles south of Dodge. Bat Masterson and Bill Tilghman entered a primitive store and saloon there and asked the patrons inside if a lone rider had passed through. No one had seen a rider matching Kenedy's descrip-tion. Wyatt and Charlie surveyed the area outside, but Kenedy wasn't around. A rumor was circulating around Dodge before the lawmen left that Kenedy might not return to Texas but ride on to Wyoming. Char-lie suggested they contact the sheriff of Cheyenne and ask him to be on the lookout for the fugitive. Masterson didn't agree. Tilghman believed Kenedy would follow the Arkansas River west and cut across the Texas Trail to join the Jones and Plummer Trail. It was decided that the posse would follow the same route.[13]

Twelve hours after he killed Dora Hand, Kenedy was on the run and being pursued by men who knew the creeks, ranches, and the wil-derness beyond Dodge City better than some of the natives. The posse was determined to apprehend the outlaw. The first day out, they traveled seventy-five miles. They considered the idea that Kenedy might have crossed the river, and they were looking for a place along the shoreline to safely lead their mounts to the other side. A heavy storm overtook them the following day. It delayed the pursued and the pursuers. Once the rain cleared, the search resumed, and by Saturday afternoon the posse was riding toward a ranch near Meade City, thirty-five miles southwest of Dodge City.[14]

The ranch house was made of sod, solidly built, with a cross-timbered roof and deep windows. A small, inviting porch extended across the front of the building, and smoke curled out of a chimney and hovered over a nearby corral. A dog barked excitedly as the horsemen slowly rode toward the house and dismounted. Just as the men stepped onto the porch, the owner of the homestead opened the front door slightly and peered out. Bat introduced the posse and himself to the man and pushed the lapel back on his duster to show the badge hanging off his vest. After studying the lawmen for a moment, the apprehensive rancher inched the door open a little farther.

"You're a long way from Dodge, ain't you?" he asked.

"We're looking for a man," Bat told him flatly.

"And you trailed him here?" the man inquired curiously.

"Have you seen anyone passing through?" Bill pressed, in a kind but firm tone.

The rancher nodded. "Yesterday," he replied, "before the storm . . . and he seemed in a hurry too."[15]

Bat glanced over at the posse's worn-out rides and carefully considered the next course of action.

"We're going to hold up here for a bit," he informed the homesteader. "Help yourself," the man said. Charlie and Wyatt returned to the horses and removed the saddles from the backs of their tired animals. Bat and Bill stood guard, eyeing the surroundings for anything that moved. Darkness slowly crept over the cattle farm, and somewhere off in the near distance a coyote yapped.[16]

Believing Kenedy had become disoriented by the storm and would surely come back by the ranch on the way toward the river, in search of a place to ford, the posse decided to stay put the following day. They left their horses unsaddled and grazing on the plain to avoid any appearance of a sheriff's posse. The lawmen all suspected they were there ahead of

Kenedy, but were prepared to catch any rider who happened onto the area exhibiting any signs of distress. Their patient waiting was rewarded by late Saturday afternoon when a solitary horseman appeared on the distant plain, approaching the ranch.[17]

Bat was hunkered down behind a cluster of boulders several hundred yards from the ranch house when he saw the rider. Settled on either side of him, but spaced fairly well apart, were the other members of the posse. Their carbine rifles ready for use, Bat, Charlie, and Bill scanned the brush, scattered rocks, and mounds from left to right. Wyatt surveyed the area with his binoculars. No one said a word as they watched the rider slowly approach.[18]

"That's Kenedy," Bat told the men, "I know him by the way he rides." Wyatt looked through his binoculars and brought the rider who was pointing his horse straight at the posse into focus. "He's right," Wyatt assured Charlie and Bill.

Kenedy urged his horse into a slight gallop, and the animal lifted his tired but proud head as he moved. His widespread nostrils greedily gulped the chilly air. For the moment, nothing seemed out of the ordinary to the fugitive. There wasn't a hint of hesitation in their approach.[19]

Kenedy squirmed uncomfortably in the saddle and slowed his horse from a fast trot to a walk. The renegade's attention was fixed on the countryside that unrolled before him. There were miles and miles of open range as far as he could see. The sky directly above was clear, with fuzzy pinches of cotton-like clouds scattered here and there, but dark thunderheads were piling up a few miles out. He led his horse around the bones of a buffalo that had fallen some time prior to his passing through the area, and the horse balked and snorted. The mount was apprehensive about moving forward. James strained his eyes over the rugged trail but failed to see anything that warranted the horse's

KANSAS STATE HISTORICAL SOCIETY

Mayor James Kelley.

obstinate behavior. He poked the animal with his spurs, and the horse continued on.[20]

Bat peered over the mound of earth he and the other posse members were positioned behind and watched the fugitive they'd been pursuing slowly draw nearer.

"We'll stop him out here," Wyatt announced. "I don't think he'll make a fight. Most likely he'll run for it." "If he does . . . I'll drop him," Charlie promised. "Kelley wants Kenedy alive," Bill reminded the men.[21]

Charlie looked around for their horses and noted that the animals were scattered about the vicinity—too far away for the lawmen to reach without being seen. "Damn it," Bat spat under his breath, realizing along with Wyatt and Bill the location of their mounts. "I'll attend to the man," Bat told his fellow riders after contemplating the distance a bullet would have to travel to hit Kenedy. "If he runs, shoot his horse," Bat ordered Wyatt.[22]

Kenedy rode on, lost in thought. The closer he got to the acres of pastureland outlining the sod house, the more nervous his horse became. The animal raised his head and neighed. Kenedy surveyed the region and again saw nothing out of the ordinary. He kept going but stopped every few yards to make sure the way was clear. Seventy-five yards away from the posse's location, Kenedy brought his ride to a stop.[23] He could hear only the cold wind blowing over the withered grass.

He scrutinized the prairie for a third time and noticed four rider-less horses milling about. Anxiety swelled to fear, and he broke out in a cold, clammy sweat. A charged silence fell over the area as the outlaw and the posse held their positions like graven images, waiting for some-one to make a first move. Kenedy's face was bloodless, and, in one quick, simultaneous motion, he removed his gun from its holster and swung his horse around.

Wyatt, Bat, Charlie, and Bill jumped up and leveled their weapons at Kenedy. "Halt," Bat shouted, cocking his weapon. Kenedy was defi-ant. He fired a shot at the same time he dug his spurs into his mount's sides.[24] The animal launched into a hard gallop. "Halt," Wyatt warned the killer again. Kenedy refused. "Last chance, Kenedy," Wyatt warned, "Halt!" Kenedy raised his whip to strike and urge his horse to go faster, but a bullet fired from Bat's .50 caliber rifle struck his left arm, and he dropped the quirt.[25] Thoroughly spooked by the violent exchange, the horse hurried to escape the scene. The lawmen let loose a volley of shots. Wyatt took careful aim and fired at Kenedy's horse. Three bullets brought the animal down. James fell out of the saddle just as his mount received the fatal shot. The horse landed hard on top of him, crushing the arm that had just been wounded. Horse and rider lay motionless on the ground.

Guns still at the ready, the posse cautiously made its way to the injured outlaw. Kenedy was writhing in pain when the lawmen reached him. The racehorse he was riding was dead, and Kenedy was unable to pull himself out from under the animal. When the police officers reached the fugitive, they spread out around him. Charlie retrieved the two .44 caliber revolvers Kenedy had dropped when he fell. Bill inspected the man's wound while Bat and Wyatt looked on.[26]

"Did I get that bastard Kelley?" Kenedy asked, his face working with insane rage. "No, but you killed someone else," Wyatt told him. "Dora Hand was asleep in Kelley's bed." Kenedy was stunned by the news. His eyes slowly filled with torment and deep regret. He glanced over at his bleeding shoulder and then looked up at the rifle in Bat's hand. "You damn son-of-a-bitch!" he said, his voice sick with anguish. "You ought to have made a better shot than you did." "Well," Bat replied with great contempt, "you damn murdering son-of-a-bitch, I did the best I could."[27]

Bat bent down to pry James from beneath the horse. Wyatt, Charlie, and Bill raised the animal on one side, and Kenedy attempted to wriggle out. Bat grabbed the criminal's wounded arm and jerked the man free. The bones in his arm crunched loudly, and Kenedy winced in pain. "You sons-of-bitches!" he shouted. "I'll get even with you for this."

Ignoring his remarks, Bat and Wyatt clamped a hand on each of his arms and pulled him up on his feet. "Which one of you shot my damn horse?" Kenedy demanded. "I did," Wyatt confessed remorsefully. "I hated to do it . . . but only because it was a beauty."[28]

The lawmen led the outlaw back to the sod ranch house where they bound and set Kenedy's shattered arm in a makeshift splint.[29] Blood from the rifle ball lodged in his shoulder had saturated his shirt. His

Wyatt Earp. KANSAS STATE HISTORICAL SOCIETY

captors had no sympathy for him. Kenedy had no sympathy for himself. He was horrified that he had killed a woman and further distressed by who it was. As Bat gruffly secured his prisoner on a pack mule the ranch owner had loaned the posse, Kenedy fought off an overwhelming wave of emotion. Unconsciously, a smothered groan escaped him. "Dora's dead," he muttered sadly.

The posse mounted their horses and guided their animals in the direction of Dodge City.

On October 6, 1878, townspeople and homesteaders conducting business at the various feed stores and shops in Dodge City stopped what they were doing to watch the posse parade down the street with its prey. Disgusted, Kenedy looked around at the curious faces. It was evident by the way he sat his horse that he was in terrible pain. The temporary bandages and splint wrapped around his arm were soaked through with blood.[30]

Bat led the way to the sheriff's office with Kenedy and the mule he was riding in tow. When the lawmen reached the jail, they dismounted, but the captured outlaw didn't make any attempt to get off his mount. His injury was so severe he couldn't lift himself out of the saddle. Tired and frustrated, Bat jerked the man off the horse. Kenedy yelped in pain.

"You should have killed me," he said to Bat with a groan.

"Don't think I didn't consider it," the lawman snapped back.

Bill escorted the criminal into the jail, and the other lawmen followed closely behind. James was deposited into a cell where he collapsed onto a rickety bunk, crying and clutching his arm. Wyatt locked him in, and Charlie sent William Duffy to get a doctor. Bat watched the deputy walk up the street by the Lone Star Saloon.

The intrepid posse's return to Dodge with James Kenedy was the topic of conversation at every saloon, barbershop, hotel, and livery stable in town. The focus of conversation centered on the so-called trap the lawmen had set to apprehend Kenedy. Newspaper accounts about what transpired were at odds with the actual event. Reports indicated that the lawmen anticipated the fugitive's every move and lured him to the homestead near the ford, making it appear as though they were not in the vicinity. The October 12, 1878, edition of the *Dodge City Times* noted that the "officers were lying in wait at Meade City, their horses unsaddled and grazing on the plain, the party avoiding the appearance of a sheriff's posse in full feather, believing that they were in advance of the object of their search, but prepared to catch any stray straggler that exhibited signs of distress."[31]

News about the lawmen's dramatic pursuit of James Kenedy spread throughout the state. According to Wyatt Earp's biographer, Stuart Lake, the publicity prompted several people to travel to Dodge to "see the intrepid officers for themselves." Legend has it that among those people was the famous publisher and dime novelist, Ned Buntline. Buntline was reportedly so affected by the posse's bravery that he commissioned the Colt manufacturing company to make special guns for each one of them.[32]

Less than two weeks after James Kenedy was arrested, Judge R. C. Cook deemed the accused was well enough to stand trial. One at a time, the posse members converged at the sheriff's office where the trial was set to take place.[33] Kenedy was escorted into the makeshift courtroom looking tired and uncomfortable. His arm was heavily bandaged and held tightly in place by a sling fashioned around his neck. His movements were feeble and slow and caused him excruciating pain. Judge Cook was not a man to be swayed by sickness or injury. He relied on proper marshaling of the facts. The plaintiff had the burden of supplying evidence to justify a conviction. Law enforcement testified to James Kenedy's suspicious behavior the night of Dora Hand's murder and recounted his confession when he was arrested. No other witnesses appeared at the hearing.

Several hours after the trial began, Charlie, Bill, Bat, and Wyatt filtered out of the building onto a relatively quiet street. The general activity around Dodge City had slowed while the hearing was in session. Some of the townspeople were milling about the thoroughfare and shop entrances, awaiting a verdict. The four lawmen were frowning, but they said nothing to the citizens eagerly hoping for news. The door to the sheriff's office opened, and James Kenedy's lawyers escorted their wounded client outside.[34]

The murmur of the men's voices and the thud of their boots on the plank sidewalk made a rippling current of sound along the block. The intrepid posse's members watched in disgust as Kenedy was led away from the jail. The look of displeasure the freed man saw on the police officers' faces pleased him. He smiled smugly as his attorneys helped him down the street toward the Dodge City Hotel. Judge Cook emerged from the office and watched Kenedy walk away. He exchanged a somber look with the lawmen, then headed off in the opposite direction of that taken by Kenedy and his representatives.[35]

Taken aback by the outcome of the hearing, the townspeople solemnly continued on with their daily business. The posse members remained where they were for a moment, uncertain about what to do next. "There wasn't anyone," Wyatt said bitterly, "to champion the cause of Dora, who was without money or influence."[36] Scowling, he strode away from the building. One by one the others left the site as well.

The October 29, 1878, edition of the *Dodge City Times* reported that James Kenedy was released due to "insufficient evidence." The article read: "Kenedy, the man who was arrested for the murder of Fannie Keenan [aka, Dora Hand], was examined before Judge [R. G.] Cook, and acquitted . . . We do not know what the evidence was, or upon what ground he was acquitted.

But he is free to go on his way rejoicing whenever he gets ready."[37]

Many of the Dodge City residents were outraged by James Kenedy's release. There was speculation that some of Mifflin Kenedy's rich associates had furnished his son with the capital necessary to retain his high-priced attorneys.[38] The general consensus was that when Mifflin got to Dodge, he would reward his loyal friends monetarily or with future political endorsements.

None of the posse members were able to determine the exact reason behind what seemed to be such a flagrant miscarriage of justice. The idea that money and position could influence the court appalled them and altered their views of police work. Wyatt admitted the outcome of James Kenedy's hearing left him disillusioned with law enforcement.[39] He grew even more embittered when the city council cut the police force's salary less than a month after Kenedy was released.

Wyatt continued to do his job with the same efficiency and courage as always, but with less patience than he had had at one time. His name slipped from the local newspapers as his faith in the work continued to diminish, but an altercation with three drunken men traveling from Leadville, Kansas, to Missouri did put Wyatt back on the front page. The lawman arrested the men and was transporting them to jail when one of them pulled a gun and attempted to shoot him.

According to the May 10, 1879, edition of the *Dodge City Times*, "While Assistant Marshal Earp was attempting to disarm [them] and [was] leading an unruly cuss off by the ear, another one of the party told his chum to 'throw lead,' and endeavored to resist the officer. Sheriff Bat Masterson soon happened on the scene and belabored the irate Missourian, using the broadside of his revolver over his head. The party was disarmed and placed in the cooler."[40]

Eleven days later, Wyatt was asked to serve a court order on a Texas drover who refused to pay one of his hands for the work he had done. Accompanied by fellow officer Jim Masterson, Wyatt presented the writ to the cattleman and his six herders. At first they resisted the lawmen, but the officers stood up to the hostile men, and the debt was promptly paid.[41]

These two volatile, publicized events, along with the outcome of James Kenedy's case, hastened Wyatt's departure from Dodge. "I'd had a belly full of lawing," he recalled later in his memoirs.[42]

Members of the most intrepid posse ever formed.

Rather than leave the profession at that time, Bat Masterson sought to change the system from within. He was interested in politics and attended Republican conventions as a Ford County delegate. He maintained his position as sheriff while waiting for his political career to take off.[43]

According to the December 10, 1878, edition of the *Ford County Globe*, the personal disappointment he experienced as a result of James Kenedy being set free in October was followed by a professional setback in December.[44] Four prisoners managed to escape from Bat's jail. Dodge City residents who didn't like the sheriff, as well as some Texas cowboys who held a grudge against him, suggested the jailbreak was allowed to happen because the inmates were Bat's friends. Bat denied the claim and immediately left town with his deputy to apprehend the fugitives. Two of the four men were eventually recaptured, their apprehension being reported in the *Ford County Globe* on March 18, 1879.[45]

Ford County commissioners who disapproved of the stern way Bat dealt with unruly cowhands; a parade of guilty thieves and murderers, who had been arrested and escaped justice; and, eventually, being voted out of office took their toll on his perception of law enforcement. Less than two years after Dora Hand was killed, Bat was making plans to relocate and pursue another career.[46]

Charlie Bassett's first term as marshal of Dodge City had been filled with tragedy and disenchantment. It started in April 1878 with the murder of Ed Masterson and concluded a year after Dora's untimely demise. The efficiency of his administration was recognized by the Ford County district court in January 1879. As reported in the *Dodge City Times*, on January 11, the court noted that "the large criminal calendar suggests the 'probability' of an 'endeavor' on the part of the officers to do their duty.

"To an unprejudiced person somebody has been making things lively. Sheriff Bat Masterson, Under Sheriff [*sic*] and Marshal Bassett, and Deputies [William] Duffy and [James] Masterson, have evidently earned the high praise accorded to them for their vigilance and prompt action in the arrest of offenders of the law."[47]

Given the discouraging result in the case against James Kenedy, Charlie considered the praise disingenuous. Nonetheless, he remained dedicated to police work until his resignation from office in October 1879.[48]

Bill reacted to the release of James Kenedy by poring over the more than fifty volumes of law books at the county prosecutor's office. His concern over the letter of the law baffled many of his cohorts, but his knowledge of the state and federal mandates aided his being appointed city marshal. Rowdy cowhands and aspiring criminals who misinterpreted his respect for the law as weakness and challenged his authority learned quickly that Bill was fearless. He disarmed many trail-stained strangers who threatened to shoot him or anyone else who lived in Dodge.[49]

Dodge City was a town tailored to fit the needs of range hands and soldiers hungry for pleasure and eager to forget hardships. There was an abundance of businesses that supplied drink, women, and games to help them do just that. The topic of Dora Hand's untimely death was soon replaced with conversation about the best places at which to spend the money that burned the fingers of men eager to turn their passions loose after long aching months of toil and sweat and cold and suffering on the plains.[50]

For a while, another criminal shifted law enforcement's attention away from James Kenedy. Henry Bourne, also known as Dutch Henry, was a murderer, mail robber, and horse thief. The outlaw had made a name for himself in several states. In January 1879, as reported on January 25, by the *Dodge City Times*, he was arrested in Colorado, and Bat Masterson had him extradited to Dodge City to stand trial for stealing horses. The trial lasted two days, and, in the end, Dutch was found not guilty. The jury cited "insufficient evidence" as the reason for acquittal. For the members of the intrepid posse, the acquittal was a jarring reminder of what had happened to Dora Hand's accused murderer.[51]

MANAGEMENT PRINCIPLES LEARNED FROM THE POSSE AFTER TIBURCIO VASQUEZ

EMBRACE ASSIGNMENTS.
When Governor Newton Booth appointed the tough, respected Alameda County sheriff Harry Morse to recruit a band of deputies to bring down Tiburcio Vasquez, Morse wasted no time in selecting the men who would be a part of the posse. All of the men were exceptional bandit hunters and couldn't wait to get to work.

DEVELOP A STRATEGIC PLAN.
While most managers agree that strategic planning can provide a road map to drive business growth and survival—and success—many fail to devote the necessary time and energy to creating such a plan. Sheriff Morse and the posse after Tiburcio Vasquez spent weeks planning the manhunt. They calculated the best time of the year to set out to find the bandit and hired spies to keep them informed of the outlaw's activities.

EXPECT SETBACKS TO HAPPEN.
There is a universal truth that a person's reaction is based on his or her expectations. Sheriff Morse was a seasoned professional who had been a part of several posses prior to forming the group who would trail Vasquez. When the posse was overcome with bad weather, he pressed on. His plan for dealing with the interruption to the hunt was to press on until they came across a clue that would lead them to the desperado. Deviating from the route traveled was not an option. Staying the course was the objective, regardless of any problems that might arise.

GET EXPERT SUPPORT AND GUIDANCE.
Two heads are better than one. Seek out experts in your network that you can call on as a lifeline when you are going through a difficult trial. Sheriff Morse called on an informant named Alfonso Burnham to help him infiltrate Vasquez's gang and lead the posse to the criminal. Once Burnham learned Vasquez's plans, he reported back to the posse. Without Burnham, locating the bandit would have taken the lawmen even longer.

FIND AND UTILIZE UNLIKELY SOURCES.
One of the men recruited to be a member of the posse after Tiburcio Vasquez was a journalist with an amazing ability to handle a gun. It was this journalist who finally stopped Vasquez from getting away. Had Sheriff Morse been set on only hiring lawmen or former lawmen to help with the search for the dangerous criminal, Vasquez's reign of terror might have been allowed to continue on.

CHAPTER FIVE

ALWAYS PLAN FOR SETBACKS: THE POSSE AFTER TIBURCIO VASQUEZ

A light, frigid rain tapped the dirty windows of a small store located along the banks of the San Joaquin River near the town of Millerton, California. A half-dozen ferryboat operators were inside soaking up the warmth emanating from a fireplace. Four of them were huddled around a table playing cards; the other two were enjoying a drink at a makeshift bar, while an unkempt clerk arranged a row of canned goods across a warped shelf.[1]

The clerk was entertaining the preoccupied men in the room with a song when the shop door swung open. He was the last to notice the figures standing in the entranceway. He looked up from his work after being conscious of his own loud voice in the sudden silence. He slowly turned to see what everyone else was staring at.[2]

The outlaw Tiburcio Vasquez entered the store with his pistol drawn. Three other desperadoes, all brandishing weapons, followed closely behind. Vasquez, a handsome man of medium height with large, dark eyes, surveyed the terrified faces of the patrons as he smoothed down his black mustache and goatee. "Put up your hands," he ordered the men. The clerk quickly complied, and the others reluctantly did the same.[3]

Two more of Vasquez's men burst into the store through the back entrance and leveled their guns on the strangers before them.[4]

"You don't need a gun here," the clerk tried to reason with the bandits.

Vasquez grinned as he walked over to the man. "Yes, I do," he said, as he placed his gun against the clerk's temple. "It helps quiet my nerves."[5]

Vasquez demanded the men drop to the floor, facedown. After they had complied, their hands and feet were tied behind them. One of the men cursed the desperadoes as he struggled to free himself. "You damned bastard," he shouted at Vasquez. "If I had my six-shooter, I'd show you whether I'd lie down or not."[6]

The bandits laughed at the outburst and proceeded to rob the store and its occupants of $2,300. The November 10, 1873, holdup was one of more than one hundred such raids perpetrated by the thirty-eight-year-old Mexican and his band of cutthroat thieves and murderers in their violent careers. The desperadoes escaped the scene of the crime, eluding authorities for several months before they were caught.[7]

Prior to the Gold Rush, California's population was composed primarily of the original Spanish and Mexican settlers and indigenous Native Americans. News of the riches found in the foothills of the territory loosed a flood of white settlers into the area. In the pioneers' quest to tame the Wild West and transform the fertile California frontier into a "civilized" state, native Californians were forced into a new way of life. Families like Tiburcio Vasquez's harbored a great deal of animosity toward the Anglo miners and businessmen who demanded that the original residents conform to their laws and way of living. Vasquez resented such treatment, and from an early age began rebelling against what he called the "gringos'" influence.[8]

Born in Monterey County, California, on August 11, 1835, Tiburcio was one of six children. His mother, Maria, was the daughter of explorer Jose Guadalupe Contua. His father, Jose, was a farmer who struggled to provide for his wife and family. Homesteaders from the East encroached on his land, making it difficult for him to compete for a share of the agricultural market. When Tiburcio was old enough to contribute financially, he took the only job he believed he could find—that of a cattle rustler and horse thief. He justified his outlawry by blaming the "Americans" for his lack of employment opportunities.[9]

When he was fifteen, he and an American boy exchanged heated words over a beautiful Mexican girl at a party both had attended. The quarrel escalated into a fistfight. The acting sheriff of Monterey was called to break up the scuffle. Vasquez was enraged by the interruption. He pulled a knife on the officer and stabbed him to death. He fled the scene and hid in the mines at Sonora, a favorite refuge for Mexican outlaws. Several attempts were made by law enforcement to apprehend Vasquez.[10]

At the age of seventeen, Vasquez went into business with a friend, using his ill-gotten gains to become the co-owner of a dance hall. The fandango proved to be profitable, but it was not without its share of problems. The settlers who frequented the place badly treated the Mexican women who worked there, calling them names and insulting their ethnicity. Their actions further fueled the hatred Vasquez had for them.[11]

Many wealthy Mexicans did not share Vasquez's opinion of the Americans. They disapproved of his criminal activities and refused to associate with him. One particular rancher, aware that his only daughter was romantically involved with the teenage bandit, forbade him from seeing her. When Vasquez disobeyed the order and kidnapped the man's daughter, the outraged rancher pursued the pair. The defiant young man refused to give up the girl; her father pulled a gun on him, and a gunfight broke out. Vasquez turned his paramour over only after he was shot in the arm.[12]

Shortly after Vasquez's arm had mended, he was involved in another confrontation, this time with a constable. The dispute resulted in the death of the lawman.[13]

The precocious young criminal eventually left Sonora and his companions at the saloon to join forces with another California bandit named Joaquin Murrieta. After the death of Joaquin, eighteen-year-old Vasquez became the acknowledged head of the outlaw forces; his intelligence, boldness, and the absolutely unscrupulous methods he used made him a formidable criminal leader.[14]

Many attempts were made by law enforcement officers of various counties to catch Vasquez, and more than once they cornered him only to have him slip away. His intimate knowledge of the country helped him, and the speed of his splendid horses frequently saved him from capture. Accompanied by several like-minded outlaws, Vasquez went on to rob numerous stores and lone travelers in Northern California.[15]

Authorities apprehended the bandit in 1857. Vasquez was brought before a judge and jury, but nothing beyond horse stealing could be proven against him. He was sentenced to five years in San Quentin. After serving less than two years, he headed a party of escaping convicts. He was quickly recaptured and held until the expiration of his term in 1863. When he left San Quentin again, he was a free, but not reformed, man.[16]

Vasquez gathered together another group of bandits and started robbing stagecoaches traveling between San Francisco and Los Angeles. He and his fellow desperadoes murdered numerous men during their holdups and gunned down any lawmen that tried to stop them.[17]

One of the most heinous crimes committed by Vasquez and his men occurred in August 1873. The band of six outlaws robbed Snyder's store located in the village of Tres Pinos in Monterey County. The store was a stage stop and post office and supplied a sparsely settled area on the road to and from San Francisco and the southern mines. Besides the store, Tres Pinos boasted a small wooden hotel, a stable for the stage teams, and a blacksmith shop. Vasquez and his followers arrived in town at seven o'clock in the evening. There were a half-dozen men in Snyder's store when they overtook it. The store clerk and five others who lived and worked in the area were ordered to toss their weapons aside and lie down on the floor. The victims did as they were told, and the bandits tied their hands behind their backs.

Vasquez and four of his cohorts began relieving the store of money and supplies; two others positioned themselves outside the building to alert their fellow robbers if someone was coming. The men guarding the store called out to Vasquez when they saw a sheepherder approaching the property. Vasquez called out in English for the man to stop, but the gentleman was Portuguese and didn't understand him. The sheepherder continued on toward the store, unaware of what was taking place inside. Before he reached the entrance of the business, Vasquez shot the man in the head.[18]

A freight teamster named Haley was the next to arrive. As he drove in front of the store and climbed down from his wagon, Vasquez came up suddenly on him and demanded that he drop to the ground. Haley was defiant and would not comply. Vasquez struck him hard across the head with the butt of his pistol, knocking him out cold.[19]

A second teamster, George Redford, saw the trouble as he rode into town. He and Vasquez exchanged a look that let George know he was not safe. He jumped off the rig and started running toward the stable. Vasquez shot him in the back before he reached the building.[20]

A blacksmith by the name of Scherrer saw what happened and made a beeline for the hotel to warn the owner and patrons to keep out of sight. The owner rushed to the front door to close and lock it. Vasquez witnessed the activity and fired a barrage of shots at the door. The hotel owner was dead by the time he hit the floor.

After taking everything of value, the bandits rode off into the night. The terrorized community was outraged by Vasquez's savagery, and an $8,000 reward was offered for his capture.[21]

COURTESY OF THE CALIFORNIA HISTORY ROOM, CALIFORNIA STATE LIBRARY, SACRAMENTO, CALIFORNIA

Tiburcio Vasquez.

Undeterred by the swarm of lawmen and bounty hunters on their trail, Vasquez and his ever-growing number of cohorts continued their crime spree, holding up a number of stores and stages in the San Joaquin Valley. One of the most ruthless of those robberies occurred in the town of Kingston. Vasquez attacked the hamlet in the dead of night and ordered his gang to tie up all the male citizens. One by one he stripped them of their personal possessions and money and then cleaned out the stores and hotels.[22]

California citizens were furious over the outlaw's violent raids and at the inability of law enforcement officers to stop him. Governor Newton Booth responded to his constituents' cry for justice and appointed the tough, respected, Alameda County sheriff Harry Morse to recruit a band of deputies to bring down Vasquez. Booth appropriated $5,000 to get the job done.[23]

Governor Booth initially instructed Sheriff Morse to lead a band of thirty men to track Vasquez. The sheriff, who had a reputation for being a relentless and resourceful man hunter, refused, arguing that a posse that size could neither ride fast enough or go undetected. The sheriff wanted a posse of eight men only.

Among the men he selected for the mission was San Joaquin County sheriff Tom Cunningham. Cunningham was recognized as being the best bandit hunter in the West, as well as a master of disguise. He could change his looks and mannerisms to gain access into criminals' hideouts and arrest outlaw ringleaders. The sheriff's eighteen-year-old son, George, an excellent shot and superior horseman, and two of his closest friends were selected as part of the posse, too. One, Ralph Faville of Pleasonton, Alameda County, was for many years a deputy under Sheriff Harry Morse. Faville was noted for his success in hunting cattle thieves and desperadoes. The second of George's friends chosen to ride with the group was A. J. McDavid of Sunol, a veteran hunter, wagon driver, and splendid shot. Rounding out the rest of the posse were Fresno County deputy sheriff Harry Thomas; Ambrose Calderwood; A. B. "Boyd" Henderson, an expert rifleman and a reporter for the *San Francisco Chronicle*; and ex-convict Ramon Romero, an exceptional traveler who was well liked by law enforcement agents and an expert cowboy who had reportedly been a member of Joaquin Murrieta's gang. Imprisoned for murder, Romero was good with a knife and knew all the secret trails outlaws used in El Camino Viejo, La Verde del Monte, San Joaquin Valley, and the Coast Range. Sheriff Morse trusted the men in his posse with his life.[24]

The posse after Tiburcio Vasquez and his gang spent weeks planning the manhunt. They calculated the best time of the year to set out to find the bandit and hired Mexican spies to keep them informed of Vasquez's activities. Sheriff Morse and the posse began their search on March 14, 1871, at Firebaugh's Ferry in Fresno County, California.[25]

When word reached Vasquez that a highly trained posse had been formed, he decided the outlaws should disband for a while. Vasquez retreated to the Valley of the Cahuengas near Los Angeles and hid out at a friend's cabin.[26]

Heavy rains in the area hampered Sheriff Morse's hunt for the desperado. His posse spent two months and traveled some 2,700 miles before getting a lead on where Vasquez was staying. In April 1874, the posse received a telegram that told them of a robbery at the San Gabriel Mission, nine miles outside of Los Angeles. Vasquez had been the culprit, and after the attack, he had retreated into the Soledad Mountains.[27]

A woman who lived in the vicinity of the desperado's hideout offered to escort the authorities to him. In exchange for the information, the woman, who was rumored to be the expectant mother of Vasquez's child, wanted a portion of the reward. Sheriff Morse was too far away from the scene to respond in a timely fashion, and a San Diego sheriff was asked to attend to the matter. The sheriff heard what the woman had to say, but he felt she was lying about what she knew and refused to investigate the tip.[28]

Shortly after Sheriff Morse and his posse had started out after Vasquez, whom they believed to be somewhere in the Tehachapi Mountains by now, the lawmen received word that another outlaw, Juan Soto, known as the "human wildcat," had been spotted in the area near Santa Clara. The sheriff's search for Soto had begun in early January 1871. Both Soto and Vasquez shared the same hideout locations, and although they didn't work together, they robbed stages and murdered stage drivers and passengers in the same wholesale manner.[29]

Sheriff Morse and his men weren't particular about which outlaw they apprehended first; both outlaws' reigns of terror needed to be stopped. His focus on Vasquez interrupted, Morse killed Juan Soto in a shoot-out in May 1871. Shortly after the Soto matter was resolved, Sheriff Morse and his capable posse directed their full attention once again on searching for Vasquez. The outlaw rarely stayed in one place for more than a few days; he was constantly moving from one hideout to another. For more than a month, the sheriff and posse traversed the hills and flatlands between San Juan and San Francisco, looking for the fugitive and his followers. Frustrated and lacking any clue as to where Vasquez could be, Sheriff Morse decided to employ the help of a bandit who once rode with Juan Soto. Sheriff Morse owed his success hunting outlaws to his judicious use of informants.[30]

Alfonso Burnham, alias Fred Welch, was the informant Sheriff Morse had in mind. Burnham had spent time in San Quentin, and once he was released, he and the sheriff became friends. Morse had helped him find legitimate work after his incarceration, and he was grateful to the lawman for aiding in his efforts to turn his life around. Burnham agreed to assist Sheriff Morse, infiltrate Vasquez's gang, and lead the posse to the criminal.[31]

It didn't take Burnham long to fall in with the wrong crowd, who suggested he might find Vasquez near Salinas in a village called Sotoville. When Burnham arrived in town, he sought out the restaurant and tied his horse in the back of the establishment. Dinner was in full swing, and the business was crowded. He didn't immediately spot Vasquez among the many patrons on hand, but just as he was about to sit down at a table, he heard a familiar voice calling his name. Vasquez was seated in a far corner of the room with several others.[32]

Vasquez signaled Burnham with a wineglass. The contents spilled on the table and floor as he motioned for Burnham to sit next to him. According to Burnham's remembrance of the occasion, he paid close attention to the man opposite Vasquez, named Procopio. Procopio was the nephew of Joaquin Murrieta, a particularly violent individual who had participated in a number of killings with Vasquez. "At all cost I must throw myself into the part," Burnham recalled telling himself as Vasquez greeted him.[33]

After pleasantries were exchanged and they had shared a meal, Burnham told Vasquez that he was on the run for killing a man in Marin. Vasquez promised Burnham he would help him get away from the authorities. Burnham agreed and headed into the mountains with Vasquez's gang. It never occurred to Vasquez that Burnham was working with the authorities when he asked to join the group.[34]

Once Burnham managed to infiltrate the gang of desperadoes and learned of their future plans, he was to get word to Sheriff Morse. The posse could then lie in wait for the criminals to fall prey to their ambush. The trouble was that Burnham was being closely watched by the outlaws, and he wasn't able to break away from the group. It wasn't until Vasquez and his men ran low on supplies and Burnham volunteered to ride to Salinas to get provisions that he was able to slip away and get a message to the sheriff about where the hideout was and what Vasquez's next move would be.[35]

Burnham had no way of knowing that Sheriff Morse and his posse would not be at the sheriff's office and subsequently not receive the telegram he sent. When the sheriff didn't hear from Burnham, he assumed something had gone wrong and resumed the search for Vasquez. When Burnham did not return to the outlaw's camp, Vasquez suspected he had been arrested by Sheriff Morse. Vasquez was aware that the sheriff and his highly skilled posse were looking for him. As the majority of the Mexicans in and around Monterey were sympathetic to Vasquez, they would not cooperate with law enforcement to assist in finding the bandit. They would, however, keep Vasquez informed of when the sheriff was nearing his camp.[36]

Vasquez and his bandits were intimidated by Sheriff Morse and had an almost superstitious dread of him. They referred to the unshakable, relentless lawman as the "beardless boy." Sheriff Morse was a quiet, modest gentleman in his demeanor—fastidiously clean-shaven and neatly dressed, except when he was on a manhunt. During those times he would sometimes assume disguises that rendered him in personal appearance more like a wandering panhandler than a lawman.[37]

Stories about how Morse stalked and captured cattle rustlers were legendary. According to the tales, Sheriff Morse possessed incredible strength and was able to snap the necks of cattle thieves in half. He had deep, piercing eyes that could see through to a man's soul. He would ride with a posse to hunt a man down but wasn't afraid to take on the job alone.[38]

George Beers, a reporter for the *San Francisco Chronicle*, wrote extensively about Sheriff Morse and his adventures. As a member of the sheriff's posse that sought Vasquez, Beers was present when accounts of the lawman were shared. One such adventure took place in 1870. Sheriff Morse was on the trail of Mexican cattle thieves suspected to be hiding in the hills of San Leandro and along the Alameda Creek.[39]

Walking stooped over with a limp and wearing a set of gray whiskers and old, tattered clothes, Sheriff Morse wandered casually into a camp he believed was that of the six cattle bandits. The outlaws were settling into their bedrolls for the evening when the sheriff, looking like Rip Van Winkle, strolled toward the campfire and asked for a cup of coffee, in Spanish. The bandits were so shocked by the behavior of what they thought was an old man, they could barely process what they were seeing.[40]

Sheriff Morse was granted permission to pour himself a cup of coffee. He then sat down across from the thieves and began telling them about his trek through the area in search of gold. He droned on for almost an hour. The criminals were only half listening as they continued to make themselves ready to get to sleep. Their guard was completely down when the sheriff stood up, pulled a pair of six-shooters out of the pockets of his duster, and leveled them at the men.[41]

The outlaws jumped to their feet, outraged and cursing, as Sheriff Morse held them at gunpoint. He stood tall now, no indication of a limp present at all. The bandits kept their hands in the air while the lawman took their weapons away from them and clasped irons around their wrists and ankles.[42]

The following morning, Sheriff Morse single-handedly escorted the rustlers to the jail at San Leandro. For a short while, cattle stealing in the hills decreased. With a reputation for being the most fearless and bravest man on the Pacific Coast, no one wanted to encounter Sheriff Morse or go against the law.[43]

By the time Sheriff Morse and the posse met up with Burnham, Vasquez and his men were long gone from the outlaw camp where Burnham had last seen them. The posse would have to consider another way to learn of Vasquez's whereabouts. Sheriff Morse decided it was time to travel to the home of Joaquin Murrieta's widow, Marianna. Procopio often visited his aunt to make sure she was doing well, and Vasquez was known to accompany him periodically. Sheriff Morse hoped Marianna could be persuaded to give the posse some information.[44]

Sheriff Morse and the posse found the forty-three-year-old widow living in the Kettleman Hills, 180 miles north of Los Angeles. She was eager to talk about her late husband, his family, and Tiburcio Vasquez after she had plenty of whiskey. She shared with the posse that she had recently seen Vasquez and he had changed his looks to travel about unfettered by law enforcement. He had shaved off his black beard, was wearing a red wig and mustache, and had blackened his lower eyelids so no one would recognize him. She told them she had overheard Vasquez say something about returning to Monterey via the trail that runs through the Santa Lucia Mountains. Sheriff Morse and the posse left Marianna alone at her camp, drinking, crying, and singing songs of remembrance of her deceased husband.[45]

Armed with the new description of Vasquez, the lawmen began exploring the Santa Lucia range, a rugged 105-mile area in coastal, central California. The area was infested with highwaymen and horse and cattle thieves. The posse split up in order to cover more ground. On April 21, 1874, Romero arrested a bandit named Nicholas Ruiz. Ruiz once rode with Vasquez and his gang, participating in a string of robberies.[46]

Romero searched Ruiz for weapons and removed the guns found on him. Among the six-shooters in his possession was a letter Ruiz was to take to the telegraph office, informing Vasquez of the movement of Sheriff Morse and his posse. Ruiz had been following the lawmen since they had arrived at Marianna Murrieta's home. Romero escorted Ruiz to Salinas where he had him placed in the custody of the local constabulary. His telegram was never sent.[47]

While in Salinas, Romero heard that Vasquez was now in Los Angeles. He managed to get word out to the rest of the posse about the outlaw's location.[48]

Sheriff Morse and the posse had been in the saddle for twenty-seven days.[49] During that time, they had thoroughly explored the difficult and, in many places, almost inaccessible wilderness in which Vasquez and his gang had their securest hiding place. They had collected a wealth of information for use if Vasquez and his men returned to the area. During the twenty-seven days, the lawmen traveled more than a thousand miles. They were frustrated, but not willing to abandon the search for Vasquez.[50]

Meanwhile, Vasquez and his men were holed up in a retreat near Soledad planning their next robbery. They were blissfully unaware that Sheriff Morse was still on their trail. The desperadoes were going to embark on an extensive raid throughout the California coast. "Vasquez thought on a grand scale," a reporter for the *San Francisco Chronicle* wrote after an interview with the ruthless bandit. "He had his eye upon a point considerably removed from his usual 'stomping ground,' where a successful robbery would put in him possession of the means to arm and equip one hundred fifty or two hundred men. With that force divided into three divisions and acting in concert, Vasquez planned to rob from businesses in all the principal towns of southern California."[51]

Vasquez gave orders to the criminals riding with him to scout the locations given to each one for ranch owners with funds that could be stolen. At the designated time, the desperadoes would overtake the property and relieve ranchers of their treasures.[52]

One of the first homes the outlaws robbed in early April 1874 belonged to an Italian sheep farmer named Repetto. Vasquez was furious to learn the rancher had little more than $80 in his possession. The only thing that kept him from being killed is that Vasquez learned Repetto had much more in the bank. He forced the rancher to sign documents relinquishing the cash held at the Temple and Workman's Bank in Los Angeles to be turned over to one of Repetto's nephews. If the nephew did not return with the funds by a certain time, his uncle would be hanged.[53]

The frightened young nephew was successful in drawing out the money, but his nervous actions aroused suspicion. The bank president alerted Los Angeles sheriff William R. Rowland of what had occurred, and the sheriff wasted no time in pulling together a posse of men he had worked with many times before. Under his command were Major H. M. Mitchell, ex-Union soldier and attorney-at-law; B. S. "Budd" Bryant, constable of El Monte; Sam Bryant, constable of Los Angeles; Tom Vincent, prospector, trapper, and an excellent marksman; George Beers of Alameda County; Sheriff Albert J. Johnson; and nine other lawmen.[54]

As soon as Repetto's nephew arrived at the ranch with the money, Vasquez took it from him and ordered his men to head back to the hideout in Soledad. He had no idea that Sheriff Morse and his posse were en route to the Soledad retreat.[55]

As Vasquez and his band of outlaws were leaving Repetto's ranch, one of the bandits with Vasquez spotted Sheriff Rowland in the far distance, following the gang. For some reason he did not tell the other bandits what he saw.[56]

A violent sandstorm halted Sheriff Morse and his posse's pursuit of the outlaws. On April 17, 1874, the lawmen reached a stage stop at Cow Spring Station, seventy-four miles northwest of Los Angeles. A driver there told them about the Repetto robbery and that Sheriff Rowland, with fifteen men, was in pursuit and traveling in the direction of Soledad. Sheriff Morse and his posse at once decided to turn around and either head off the fugitives or join in the pursuit with the Los Angeles party. From this time until the first of May, Sheriff Morse's posse scouted the mountains and canyons and guarded the trails from the San Fernando Valley to Elizabeth Lake, moving rapidly from point to point in the endeavor to cooperate with different law enforcement parties sent out from Los Angeles.[57]

Vasquez evaded the posses on every side by daring to follow narrow, difficult paths leading into deep gorges. The outlaws found patches of wild grass for their horses there and used food stolen from Repetto's supply house to keep themselves alive while making their way over the rocks and canyon trails.[58]

COURTESY OF JOHN BOESSENECKER

Sheriff Harry Morse.

On April 20, Sheriff Morse, Sheriff Rowland, and their posses met to determine who would go where next. Sheriff Morse and his men were to comb the terrain in the north along Tujunga Canyon, and Sheriff Rowland and his men would cover the south side of the canyon. On April 22, a dispatch from Los Angeles was delivered to Sheriff Rowland informing him that Vasquez had been seen near San Fernando. The lawman hurried toward the village, but found nothing. The report turned out to be false. Sheriff Rowland and Sheriff Morse rendezvoused again and decided where they should search next. The posses separated, carefully traversing through different sections of the southern portion of the state.[59]

On April 27, 1874, Sheriff Morse received information he believed was credible. Not only did he learn that Vasquez was in Los Angeles County, but a man who was once Vasquez's guide also offered to lead the lawmen to the exact house in which he was hiding. Sheriff Morse got word to Sheriff Rowland about the findings. Sheriff Rowland was kind, but doubted the veracity of the guide and refused to act on the tip. Sheriff Rowland and his posse returned to Los Angeles to decide the next course of action.[60]

On May 13, 1874, Sheriff Rowland and his posse learned through a rancher named D. K. Smith that Vasquez and his men were meeting at the home of a bandit named Greek George in Nicholas Canyon. Sheriff Rowland suspected Vasquez's spies were watching his every move and reporting what they knew to the outlaw. The lawman decided that he would stay behind and not go to Greek George's house. Major Mitchell and Constable Bryant stayed with Rowland for a few hours, then rode off to join the rest of the posse. All agreed it was the right move to make. Sheriff Rowland's absence from town would be instantly known, and the hunted bandit would be on his guard.[61]

At ten o'clock in the evening, F. Hartley, Los Angeles chief of police; W. E. Rogers of Los Angeles; Undersheriff Johnston; detective Emil Harris; and George Beers made their way to Greek George's place.[62] According to an article written by George Beers, the following plan of attack was issued.

"The arms, consisting of Henry rifles, revolvers, double-barreled shotguns, and Bowie knives, were to be boxed up and placed on a cart and conveyed by a roundabout way to Jones's corral, in the outskirts of the city. The horses should be gradually taken there from different stables, at different times, and by different routes during the night by employees of the corral. The members of the expedition were also to reach the corral, going singly, at different hours and by different routes—every man to be on hand at two [a.m.] on the 13th. To prevent any unpleasant interruption it was arranged that if any person called at the corral to procure horses, they should not be admitted, the excuse being that 'all the horses were out'; and if anyone wanted to stable an animal, the 'corral was full—no empty stalls.'

"One after another the conspirators glided like shadows through the streets, and at two o'clock the mysterious conclave had assembled. Selecting their arms—each man having indicated his preference—they mounted, and emerging from the corral slowly and silently, wended their way out of the city, and crossing the plains in a northerly direction, entered Nichols Canyon from the La Brea ranch, about a mile and a quarter east of 'Greek George's' house, and proceeded far enough up the canyon to effectually conceal themselves from view.

"At early daylight, Mitchell and Johnston left the party, and going up a side canyon, [climbed] the mountain and moved along its crest for over a mile, and then, crawling on their bellies to a point from which they could get a good view of the premises of 'Greek George,' they watched the place until nearly noon."[63]

Sometime during the long wait, Vasquez was alerted that the posse had located him and was closing in. He tried to make a run for it. Beers took aim with his shotgun and sent a volley of pellets into the bandit. Vasquez survived his injuries and was transported to Los Angeles. He was jailed and his wounds were treated. As soon as he was able to travel, the authorities loaded him aboard a steamer and escorted him to San Francisco. From there, he would be moved to San Jose, where his trial would be held. Hundreds of people flocked to get a glimpse of the outlaw.[64]

On January 6, 1875, Tiburcio Vasquez was tried in San Jose for the Tres Pinos murders. The gallery was filled with local residents, many of whom visited the criminal in his cell when the hearing concluded each day. In one evening, Vasquez received 673 visitors, the majority of them being women who saw the bandit as a folk hero.[65]

Vasquez's trial ended two months after it began. After deliberating for two hours, the jury found him guilty, and he was sentenced to hang on March 19, 1875.[66]

As he was being led to the gallows, which had been imported from Sacramento, he offered an explanation for his actions to onlookers. "A spirit of hatred and revenge took possession of me," he said. "I had numerous fights in defense of what I believed to be my rights and those of my countrymen. I believed we were unjustly deprived of the social rights that belonged to us."[67]

Just before he was executed, Vasquez turned to the lawman adjusting the noose around his neck and spoke one last word: "Pronto!" With that, the trapdoor dropped out from under the outlaw, and he fell to his death.[68]

Sheriff Harry Morse served as the sheriff of Alameda County for fourteen years. When he left office in 1878, he continued working in the law enforcement industry as the founder of the Harry N. Morse Detective Agency. It was his agency that went on to help capture another famous criminal, the poet highwayman Black Bart.

MANAGEMENT PRINCIPLES LEARNED FROM THE POSSE AFTER SAM BASS

IMPROVE YOUR ATTENTION TO DETAIL.

Don't let the big picture keep you from watching out for the small details. The posse after Sam Bass and his gang were so focused on finding the outlaw in the process of perpetrating a crime that they overlooked the criminals riding with them. Bass and one of his gang members pretended to be lawmen looking for the bandit, and the posse never thought of asking for credentials. The very idea that Bass would be out in the open was inconceivable to them. They saw him as only a train robber and couldn't imagine him in any other setting.

HIRING THE RIGHT TALENT CAN MAKE OR BREAK YOU.

When the superintendent of the Texas and Pacific Railway decided that action needed to be taken to stop Sam Bass from robbing his trains, he hired the best lawman around, Captain Junius Peak. Peak was a man of action, dedicated to making sure the railroad lost no further money.

LEAD YOUR TEAM INTO UNKNOWN LAND.

There seems to be a mythical fear when it comes to things that have never been tried or ideas that have never been explored. Following Sam Bass and his gang into a dangerous swamp might have seemed like an insane notion, but Captain Peak was sure it was the only way to apprehend the outlaws. The risk led to the capture of Sam Bass.

KNOW WHAT TO SACRIFICE.

When Captain Peak was faced with the idea of what had to be forfeited to ensure the posse got their man, he didn't hesitate. It was difficult, but there was a benefit to killing the desperadoes' horses. Something had to be given up for the sake of the greater goal.

REGROUP AND REFLECT.

When Sam Bass slipped away from the posse, Captain Peak decided it was time to take a step back and reevaluate the situation. According to *Life and Adventures of Sam Bass*, it was determined that "brains were better than eyes. The keen strategic mind runs further, faster, and more surely than the swiftest steed . . . and that robbers are not wise—they are traitors to human society." That last bit of wisdom proved to be crucial to delivering Bass into the hands of the law.

CHAPTER SIX

IT'S OKAY TO REGROUP AND REFLECT: THE POSSE AFTER SAM BASS

Nighttime overtook the Union Pacific train traveling west from Kansas City, Missouri, to Denver, Colorado, through Nebraska. The straight, single track stretched for miles over the desolate, shadeless, featureless land whose only trace of civilization was found in patches of plowed earth, rich and black, alternating with unfenced fields of young grain, and in a few lonely settlements of a half-dozen houses. It was along this section of railroad in late September 1877 that the train relaxed its headlong speed to a slower rate. It would run smoothly and steadily toward the water station of Big Springs, Nebraska. The passengers on board would get a respite from oscillating curves and erratic jolts and jars. The journey promised to be fairly uneventful, with nothing to see apart from a lone tree in the sleepy town in the far distance.[1]

Just before 10 p.m., the Union Pacific train stopped in Big Springs. Station employees were not on hand to greet the vehicle as they usually did. Three armed gunmen, Jack Davis, Sam Bass, and Joel Collins, had tied up the station agent and his assistant and locked them in a closet. Before the engineer had a chance to leave the train to find the agent, Joel Collins jumped on board brandishing a weapon and demanded the engineer and the fireman throw up their hands. The cocked six-shooter aimed at their heads persuaded them to do as they were told.[2]

With guns drawn, Sam Bass, Jack Davis, and Tom Nixon boarded the express car and were ransacking its contents when they came upon a couple of safes. One of the safes was partially opened, and a large quantity of gold was inside. The thieves took possession of the gold and turned their attention to a second safe that was locked. Jack ordered the messenger to open the safe. He informed the gunman he didn't have a key, but Jack didn't believe him. He slugged the messenger over the head with the butt of the gun and then thrust the revolver into the man's mouth, knocking out one of his teeth in the process. Jack threatened to blow the top of his head off if he didn't open the safe. All the man could do was shake his head. Sam convinced Jack the messenger was telling the truth and that they should move on.[3]

Two additional desperadoes, Bill Heffridge and James Berry, joined Sam and Jack in the coach where they proceeded to rob the terrified passengers. Once the deed was done, the gang of robbers jumped off the train and onto their awaiting horses. The gang fired off several shots at the train and rode off into the darkness. A few of the bullets found victims, but no one was killed.[4]

The gold taken from the express car amounted to the sum of $60,000. The ill-gotten gains consisted entirely of $20 gold pieces. The outlaws divided the stolen money and separated, going two different routes. Sam, Jack, and Tom went one way, Bill, James, and Joel in another.[5]

As the station agent was made to destroy the telegraph equipment before having been bound and shoved into a confined space, there was no way of reporting the robbery. A $10,000 reward was offered for the capture of Sam Bass and the other bandits with him.[6]

When Bass was growing up in Lawrence County, Indiana, he never saw himself as a train robber. He wanted to be a cowboy and possibly own his own cattle ranch. Born on July 21, 1851, to Daniel Bass and Elizabeth Sheeks, Sam was one of ten children. He had lost both of his parents by the time he turned thirteen, and shortly after his fifteenth birthday, he fell into the company of teenagers with bad character. He left Indiana and headed to St. Louis. He worked at a mill, took up gambling, and learned how to use a revolver.[7]

Sam moved to Texas in 1870 and settled in the town of Denton. He had a number of odd jobs, one of which was for a sheriff named W. F. Eagan. For a time, it seemed, he was dedicated to turning his life around. He attended church and learned to read and write. Then came the day he purchased a chestnut mare that was fast and liked to race. Sam soon abandoned all desire for honest work and chose instead to take bets on the various races in which his horse participated. The majority of the bets Sam took came from patrons at the local saloon. The company he kept was mostly criminals, petty thieves, and cattle rustlers who traveled with him to Fort Sill, Oklahoma.[8]

Bass planned to challenge Native Americans in the area to race their horses against his mare. He was confident his mount would win, and he was correct. The Indians that lost to Bass paid off in ponies. Bass was going to drive his winnings to San Antonio and sell them there. Not only did he leave the Oklahoma area with the animals he had won, but with a number of other ponies, too. This was the first act of robbery recorded in Bass's career.[9]

While in Texas, Sam Bass made the acquaintance of fellow outlaw Joel Collins. The pair was hired to round up a drove of cattle to be sold for the Northern market. The bulk of the livestock collected had been legitimately purchased, but there were just as many cattle that had brands of competing ranches. Bass and Collins decided they would re-brand the animals, sell them, and pocket the funds from the sale. The cattle drive ended in Deadwood, South Dakota. Bass and Collins used the money they received for the herd to purchase their own freight business. For a fee they hauled supplies from the Black Hills to Dodge

City, Kansas, and back again. In January 1877, the two decided to sell the business and open a gambling saloon and house of prostitution in Deadwood.[10]

In the summer of 1877, Bass made one final try at owning and operating a legitimate business. He and Collins pooled their funds and bought a quartz mine. The sellers of the mine had made the venture look promising. They salted the mine, making the inexperienced Bass and Collins believe there was a fortune to be made. The mine was worthless, and the pair was broke within six months.[11]

Bass and Collins decided to cut their losses and abandoned Deadwood. Four other men the duo had met in South Dakota left with them. The followers had all been involved in various crimes and were willing participants in the train robbery at Big Springs.[12]

As expected, the Big Springs robbery created intense excitement among railroad officials and caused a general sensation throughout the country. The large amount of money secured was looked upon as a temptation which could prompt others to follow suit. This, in connection with the heavy shipments of gold over the rail line, would be likely to excite every bandit in the West. At the same time, the long stretch of road through waste and desert regions, with here and there a lonely station, made it very difficult to afford adequate protection. It was determined, therefore, to capture the robbers at any cost, no matter what the hazards. Large rewards were at once offered by the state authorities of Nebraska and by the railroad companies. Detectives from many quarters flocked to the scene of the crime. Telegrams were sent to all officers along railroad lines and to sheriffs and officers in command of US troops.[13]

Joel Collins and Bill Heffridge were the first of the outlaws to be apprehended. One of the passengers on the train had recognized Collins as a man he knew from Deadwood. The witness was able to provide authorities with a description of Collins and some background infor-

HILLYER, H. B. [PORTRAIT OF JIM MURPHY, SAM BASS, AND "SEBE" BARNES], 1874, ABILENE PHOTOGRAPH COLLECTION AT HARDIN-SIMMONS UNIVERSITY, ABILENE, TEXAS

Sam Bass, seated in between outlaws Jim Murphy and "Sebe" Barnes.

mation. Armed with the details of the bandits, along with a rumor that Collins had been seen near Hays City, Kansas, Sheriff George Bardsley of Ellis County, Kansas, recruited a squad of ten cavalrymen and a detective from Denver to help find the thief. On September 26, 1877, Joel Collins was spotted with another gang member, Bill Heffridge, riding toward a train watering station sixty miles west of Hays City. Sheriff Bardsley and his posse overtook the criminals as they traveled along the Texas Trail.[14]

Collins and his partner seemed to go along with the arrest and agreed to ride to jail fairly easily, but, somewhere on the open prairie, the two men decided to take a stand. The pair drew their revolvers, but before they could shoot, the soldiers with the posse opened fire, killing the fugitives. A portion of the gold stolen from the train was found in the saddlebags on the outlaws' horses.[15]

News of the next member's whereabouts reached authorities in Boonville, Missouri, on October 9, 1877. James Berry had robbed the Union Pacific train with Sam Bass. Berry had been seen in the town of Mexico, Missouri, where he had sold $9,000 in gold to the bank there. He bought an expensive suit of clothes for himself and $300 worth of groceries, which were sent to his family in Callaway. While he was spending his money, the bank was routing the gold he sold them to St. Louis. Inspectors identified the gold as part of the treasure stolen by the Union Pacific robbers.[16]

A corps of detectives from St. Louis and Chicago was immediately dispatched to Mexico. Sheriff Henry Glascock of Audrain County, Missouri, was placed in charge of the highly skilled posse. There were rumors that Berry had left Mexico and was going to rendezvous with Bass and the other gang members. Sheriff Glascock sent his men to search for the criminal. He stayed behind, recruiting three more men, John Coons, Bob Steel, and Morgan Moore, to help him track Berry. All were expert riflemen and riders. After an extensive search of the farms around Mexico, Berry was found at the home of one of his friends, Bose Cazy.[17]

The sheriff and his posse surrounded the modest home and waited for Berry to make an appearance. Sheriff Glascock was the first to spot the outlaw unhitching his horse from a tree and leading the animal to a water trough. The sheriff trained his shotgun on Berry and demanded that he stop and put up his hands. Berry started to run, and the lawman fired his weapon over the criminal's head. Berry continued to run, so the sheriff fired again. Seven pieces of buckshot lodged in the outlaw's leg just below the knee. He dropped to the ground, writhing in pain. When the sheriff got to him, he was trying to get his pistol out but was unable to draw it before the lawman reached him. The sheriff snatched it away. Berry then asked the sheriff to shoot him, crying out that he didn't want to live.[18]

Berry was taken to jail, and Sheriff Glascock and posse member John Carter proceeded to the robber's home not more than ten miles away from the location where Berry had been found. The lawman hoped to recover the stolen money and speculated the outlaw might have hidden it at his home. When the sheriff and deputy arrived, Berry's wife answered the door. Glascock asked if she knew where her husband was, and she told him she had not seen him in four or five days. The sheriff then informed her that he had caught Berry and that he'd been shot, but he was alive. According to Sheriff Glascock's account of the scene in the October 18, 1877, edition of the *Mexico Weekly Ledger*, Mrs. Berry was surprised. "I never thought he would be taken alive," she confessed. "He said a good many times he would never be taken alive." Mrs. Berry and her five children wept at the news. The lawmen searched the home for money but found nothing.[19]

A physician's assistant tended to Berry's wounds, but there was little that could be done to keep gangrene from setting in. The outlaw died from his injuries at one o'clock in the morning on October 18. Before he passed away, he told Sheriff Glascock that Tom Nixon, one of the gang members who had robbed the train with him, was going to go to Chicago and then on into Canada. He either didn't know or wouldn't tell what he knew of Sam Bass.[20]

In less than a month, three of the Big Springs robbers had been located and killed. Finding the remaining three would not come as easily.[21]

When the gang of outlaws separated after holding up the train, Sam Bass and Jack Davis had headed in the direction of Sidney, Nebraska. They changed their minds at the last minute and decided to go to Texas. According to Davis, while en route to Denton, Texas, he and Bass "fell in with a company of soldiers and detectives." The men were searching for the bandits that had robbed the Union Pacific train. Bass told the riders that he and Davis were detectives looking for the same desperadoes. The group rode along together for four days. All the while, a portion of the gold that was stolen was packed away in the saddlebags draped around the necks of Bass and Davis's horses. The search party never had a clue their new friends were the crooks they were after. Finally, Bass and Davis peeled off from the party and continued south toward their destination.[22]

Bass and Davis parted ways before they reached Texas, with Davis deciding to travel to New Orleans. Bass was greeted with open arms by his friends in Denton. He appreciated their kindness and expressed his gratitude, passing out gold pieces to anyone who treated him with respect. Scoundrels and gamblers took full advantage of the outlaw's generosity, and even though they suspected Bass had acquired the gold in an illegal way, they were disinclined to make that point to the law. They liked having him around because they liked his money.[23]

By late February 1878, funds started to run short for Bass. Coincidentally, a series of new train robberies began to occur. The first was committed at Allen Station, a small place on the Houston and Texas Central Railroad, twenty-four miles north of Dallas. This robbery took place around nine or ten at night on February 22.[24]

Four masked gunmen overtook a southbound train. One outlaw jumped on the engine and subdued the engineer. The other three hurried to the express car and attempted to enter it. A messenger was standing in the door and refused to let the outlaws proceed further. "Your money or your brains," one of the masked robbers announced. The messenger drew his pistol and began shooting. The gunmen returned fire, seriously wounding the railroad employee. The outlaws removed more than $2,500 from the safe and made a quick getaway.[25]

In mid-March another Houston and Texas Central train was robbed. This time the scene was a small station named Hutchins, ten miles south of Dallas. The train selected for attack was again the southbound through express and mail train from Chicago and St. Louis, which passed the station around 10 p.m.[26]

The messenger present during the robbery at Allen Station was aboard the train stopping at Hutchins. He had survived the injuries he'd suffered in the last robbery he witnessed, was back on the job, and subject to the same treatment. This time, however, he did not challenge the thieves. He let them take the money from the safe without incident.[27]

The third attack took place on April 4, 1878, at Eagle Ford station, six miles west of Dallas. According to the April 13, 1878, edition of the *Dallas Weekly Herald*, the westbound passenger and express train on the Texas and Pacific Railway was robbed by four masked men armed with Winchester rifles.[28]

"As the train drew up to the depot, the robbers rushed into the office and made a prisoner of Mr. J. Hixcox, railroad agent," the *Dallas Weekly Herald* article read. "One of the party covering him with a pistol kept the agent in the office while the three others hurried to the locomotive and arrested the engineer and fireman, whom they marched, together with the agent, to the door of the express car.

"Before leaving the depot the agent had been ordered upon reaching the express coach to ask to be admitted, feigning as though he was alone. Although all had been done, the suspicions of the express messenger must have been aroused, for when the agent asked for admittance as he had been commanded, the messenger refused to open the door under any circumstances, informing the agent that he could only get in by breaking in the door. One of the robbers ran to the tender and, returning with a stick of wood, proceeded to batter in the door, the leader of the outlaws at the same time calling out to the messenger that they would give him two minutes to open the door.

"When the messenger opened it, he was covered with the arms of the party and ordered to unlock the safe. On entering the car, the robbers immediately went through it. This completed, the leader of the gang said, 'Well, well, now see what's in Uncle Sam's packages.' The mailbags were rifled and all registered letters were taken.

"After the robbery the maskers backed some distance from the train with their weapons presented to prevent an attack, and then turning, retreated hurriedly in a northeasterly direction."[29]

The Eagle Ford robbery infuriated residents in and around the Dallas area who were already annoyed with the criminal activity. They demanded state authorities do something besides offering a reward for the robbers' capture. While the law-abiding citizens of Texas were making their feelings known to community leaders, Bass and crew decided to try to rob another train, this time at Mesquite, a small station on the Texas and Pacific Railway a few miles east of Dallas.[30]

Although the plan for the robbery seems to have been the same as the one previously executed with so much success, this time it was ultimately hampered greatly by the bravery of the conductor and express messenger.[31]

"The train arrived at Mesquite about ten [p.m.] on April 11, 1878," an article in the April 13, 1878, edition of the *Dallas Weekly Herald* read. "Just before the train came to a stop, the conductor, Mr.

Julius Alvord, who was sitting in the sleeper when the whistle blew for the depot, stepped from the sleeper to the rear platform of the next coach. As he did he heard gunfire toward the engine, and, anticipating what was up, drew a double derringer from his pocket and fired it at a fellow with a gun in his hand, thinking that resistance would drive them away. Two men immediately opened fire on Mr. Alvord when he retreated to his sleeper to retrieve his six-shooters. On making his appearance the second time, the firing had become promiscuous. He entered into the battle, and the second and third shot from his revolver took effect on a medium-sized man, who staggered back into the darkness. The man wore a suit of brown overalls, a broad-brimmed hat, and had a very heavy, black mustache which came down over his mask.

"Alvord showed great pluck, and deserves much credit for the brave manner in which he stood the racket. After being shot he jumped under the coach and emptied his weapon at the robbers from behind the track. He lost so much blood and his wound was so painful that he returned to the sleeper, after exhausting his ammunition. Binding up his arm with a torn sheet, he bore his suffering with great coolness and heroism till he arrived in the city, where he was conveyed to a room at the Windsor Hotel and his wound dressed by Dr. L. E. Locke. At two o'clock in the morning he was resting easy.

"The engineer and fireman were taken from the engine and a guard placed over them, who required them to hold up their hands while the attack was going on; otherwise, they were not molested. The robbers immediately tried to effect an entrance to the express and mail car, which is used for both, but divided by a partition. The messenger and guard stood at their posts, however, and closed the door on them.

"The car was then saturated with coal-oil, and fifteen minutes by the watch was given the messenger to open the door, the robbers threatening to set it on fire and shoot everyone that got out, if the door was not opened.

"The messenger, whose name is Kerley, told them to fire away. The time being up, one of the gang struck a match, and proceeded to ignite the coal-oil, when, seeing all further resistance useless, the messenger and guard were covered with Henry rifles, when the robbers proceeded to rifle the mails and express packages. The messenger fought bravely, and fired on the robbers from the time the first one showed his head till he was compelled to open the door to save the train from being burned and many from being shot to death.

"Three registered letters were taken from the mail agent and about $152 from the express. There was over two thousand dollars in the car, but it was hid where they could not find it.

"It is thought that another one of the robbers was shot by one of the passengers from a window of the second-class coach.

"It is variously estimated that there were from nine to twenty men in the band of robbers. There were about twenty-five passengers on the train.

"A convict train was lying about one hundred yards from where the robbery occurred, on a sidetrack, and in the general engagement the guards fired into the robbers. In retaliation the robbers threatened to release the convicts, but did not do so.

"The robbers were masked, and when they left the express car they separated, going leisurely in every direction."[32]

The superintendent of the Texas and Pacific Railway decided that action needed to be taken. The superintendent, along with the governor, sought help from Captain Junius W. Peak, a pioneer Texan, Indian fighter, and early Texas Ranger. Captain Peak reviewed the three train robberies that had occurred and determined they had all been perpetrated by the same men, and that those men were Sam Bass and his followers, Nixon and Frank Jackson, an additional bandit who joined the group. Captain Peak organized a posse to track and arrest Bass and his gang. Among the posse members were Samuel Finely, an investigator; James Curry, a detective; Ed Smith, a telegraph operator; and William Edwards, a police officer. They made good time finding the gang's trail, which led to Denton County. Once in Denton, the posse traveled to the home of Sam Bass, but there wasn't a soul in sight.[33]

Bass and his gang had heard that a posse was riding after them, and they hid in the outskirts of town watching the lawmen's activity. Bass and his fellow bandits had been joined by more than fifty friends from Denton who were convinced the suspected outlaws were blameless. They were all ready to fight to defend Bass if it came to it. Fortunately, Captain Peak and his posse decided to continue the search for the bandits beyond Bass's home. The gang of scoundrels decided to ride toward Dallas. While en route, they planned the next robbery of the Texas and Pacific Railway. Captain Peak had plans of his own to make with posse members, who believed Bass would never stray from Denton.[34]

"Sam Bass, the railroad robber and brigand of Texas, is a hard bird to catch," noted an article in the June 9, 1878, edition of *The Times*. "Thus far he has successfully eluded capture.... The ultimate capture of Bass and his comrades is, however, only a question of time. Meanwhile he is a terror to the country he infests."[35]

The citizens of Texas had faith in Captain Peak, but their patience was wearing thin. Major John B. Jones, commander of the state police, and Captain Peak discussed the idea of using an outlaw named Will Scott to infiltrate Sam Bass's gang to find out what other robberies Bass planned to perpetrate. In exchange for full immunity, Will would join Bass's group and act as though he wanted to be a part of the band of thieves. Bass had been involved in robberies with Will years prior, so the likelihood that Sam would agree was good.[36]

TEXAS RANGERS HALL OF FAME AND MUSEUM

Captain Junius Peak.

Law enforcement's campaign against Bass and his gang officially began on April 24, 1878. According to a biography of Sam Bass's life and adventures compiled in late 1878, "More men were employed in this campaign, more powder burned, more bullets buried in post oaks and green hillsides, more horses rode to death, more ground galloped over, more false alarms given, more prophecies blown into thin air, more expectations blasted, and fewer men captured than ever before occurred in any similar campaign in history."[37]

In addition to Captain Peak's posse's search for Bass, Sheriff William F. Eagan joined the challenge with his own group of men. More than 150 highly qualified law enforcement members participated in the quest to apprehend Bass.

From Dallas, all headed to Denton County, Texas, where Bass made a habit of hiding. The reason Bass chose to stay in Denton County was in part due to the abundance of places to hide. When riders traveled through the cross timbers, they came upon elm and hickory bottoms where four or five Chickahominy swamps all boiled down into one. The foliage was dense, the vines hung in masses, and the undergrowth was thick. Bass and company knew the bottoms thoroughly.[38]

Throughout the month of May, three different groups of lawmen made attempts to venture into the treacherous swamp area to capture Bass and his gang. Witnesses had spotted the outlaws at a store purchasing supplies and crossing farmland near a cedar tree–lined area a few miles from the swamp. Gunfire was exchanged, but each time Bass and the others managed to slip away.[39]

On June 12, 1878, Captain Peak and his posse received word that Bass had been spotted in Wise County, Texas, and arriving at the scene, the rangers followed the desperadoes into the tangled wood along Salt Creek near Cottondale. The bulk of the day was spent searching through the dense bushes for the hidden robbers. In the afternoon, they were suddenly discovered lounging under the trees on the bank of the stream, their horses having been tied up in a small area a few feet away. The posse at once opened fire upon them, and the fight which ensued was the sharpest and most successful of the campaign. The bandits seemed more anxious to escape to their horses than to fight, but the posse crossed the stream and headed them off from the horses. During the fight when one of the robbers stumbled into the open, Sergeant Floyd, a crack shot, fired and killed him instantly. The victim was Arkansas Johnson, a thief from Johnson County, Missouri. Bass was standing at his side but escaped with the other thieves, unhurt.[40]

Shortly after the fall of Johnson, the robbers slipped away through the tangled wood and, escaping under the bank of the creek, concealed themselves in a large excavation. While here, as was afterwards learned, one of the posse came very near and stood plainly in view. Jackson leveled his rifle upon him and asked Bass if he should shoot. The chief said, "No, not unless he turned this way."

Tom Nixon, however, escaped to the horses, mounted one of them, and was returning when he was met by Captain Peak in the woods. The two men exchanged gunfire, and when Captain Peak shouted to the posse members following behind him, Nixon spurred his horse along quickly and got away. The heads of the robbers' horses were now seen in a clump of trees in the near distance. As Captain Peak did not know where the robbers were, and fearing they might be with the horses, he ordered his men to fire on them. The men did as ordered; two of the animals were killed, and the others were captured.[41]

With Bass and most of his outlaws on the run again, Captain Peak and his posse took a moment to regroup and reflect on their endeavors to apprehend Bass and his gang. It was determined that "traversing swamp-infested land with dense, low-hanging trees throughout the area was not recommended. Brains were better than eyes. The keen, strategic mind runs further, faster, and more surely than the swiftest steed, and that robbers are not wise—they are traitors to human society." The last bit of wisdom about outlaws would prove to be crucial to delivering Bass into the hands of the law.[42]

From June 12 through July 22, 1878, the posse Captain Peak led and the one Sheriff Eagan was in charge of managed to apprehend and arrest the robbers associated with Sam Bass. One of the gang members Captain Peak tracked down was James Murphy. Murphy was placed under arrest and was being held for trial for train robbery. He made it clear upon being locked in jail that he would do whatever was needed to get free. Captain Peak recalled that bit of information when rumors were circulating throughout north Texas that Sam Bass was planning on leaving the state and fleeing to Mexico. Law enforcement officials decided to strike a deal with Murphy. They promised to secure his release if he would betray Bass. Murphy agreed.[43]

The September 14, 1878, edition of the *San Marcos Free Press* included an article describing Murphy's actions after he was released from custody. He'd been tasked with returning to Denton County and rejoining the Bass gang in the character of a spy, with the object of giving the robbers away at the first fitting opportunity. To aid the outlaw in his venture, a report was circulated that Murphy had escaped and had "jumped his bond." Captain Peak and the other officials hoped this news would fool the robbers into thinking Murphy was a fugitive from justice.[44]

Murphy played his part well. When he finally met with the gang, he told them he had to hide out from the law and promised to assist them in all their undertakings. At first the gang was suspicious of the recruit, but Murphy did his best to win them over. The gang agreed to let Murphy ride with them to Elm Creek, a town a short distance from Dallas. The outlaws planned to spend two days at the location, resting. It was while Murphy and the others were taking a break that Bass received information that Murphy had joined the group for the sole purpose of betraying them.[45]

"For the spy it was a moment of extreme peril," the *San Marco Free Press* article noted. "But for his coolness and the efforts of a robber with the gang named Jackson, who had been raised with Murphy in the same neighborhood, all would have been lost, and Murphy's body left as food for the ravens of the valley." After Bass announced that Murphy must die, Jackson took up for Murphy, and Murphy began pleading for his life.[46]

"He confessed to Bass the whole transaction and agreement with Major Jones and other law enforcement agents, but solemnly declared his only and sole purpose was to betray, not the robbers themselves, but 'give away' Major Jones and the officers of the law, and thus make his own escape from the toils," the *San Marco Free Press* report continued. "These protestations were made with so much apparent candor that Sam Bass and the other robbers finally relented and allowed Murphy to continue with them; but they afterward kept a strict watch upon him.

"On June 15, 1878, the robbers left Elm Creek and the dense forest of Denton County. Their course was due south toward Austin, the intention of their chief being to rob some bank or train and flee to Mexico to take refuge from the Rangers and detectives. They reached Rockwall where they stayed one night. At Terrell they reconnoitered and examined the banks, but concluded the job of robbing them would not pay. They were pretty well mounted on fast horses and kept the towns along the line of the Central Railway to Ennis Station. Here Bass and Murphy took dinner at a hotel and their horses had provender at a livery stable. The chief, with practiced eyes, examined the Bank of Ennis, but concluded it would be a bad undertaking, and so the bandits continued their progress southward.

"Reaching the stirring interior city of Waco, on the Brazos terminus of a branch of the Texas Central, the bandits went to camp in some thick woods in the Brazos bottom, or, rather, swamp, two miles east of the town. Jackson and Murphy were sent in to spy out the banks. The former reported favorably on the State Savings Bank as an easy and rich prize. The chief concluded to make the attempt. Murphy, however, for obvious reasons, argued against the enterprise, holding that the place was too populous, the banisters too high, and the distance to run to their horses too great. Bass, therefore, abandoned the scheme. The chief and Murphy returned to town, and took a drink, Bass exchanging the last $20 gold piece he had remaining from the great $60,000 train robbery in Nebraska on the Union Pacific.

"The same night Barnes, one of the robbers, went into the edge of Waco and stole a horse. Continuing the journey southward, the gang struck the small town of Belton, Central Texas. Here Murphy sold Barnes' old mare, and on pretense of getting a $5 bill changed, eluded the robbers long enough to indite [*sic*] a hasty letter to Sheriff Eagan, who had, by Major Jones, been let into Murphy's secret. At Georgetown, Williamson County, not far from the village that a few days later was the scene of their chief's death-shot, the robbers made a short sojourn, but were advised by Murphy against [an] attempt to rob the bank because the safe was too far in the rear of the building.

"At Georgetown the spy managed to write Major Jones to have his men at Round Rock ready. Bass caught him in the act of mailing the letter, and demanded an explanation. The spy, however, got out of it by hard and downright lying. Keeping the road to Austin the bandits camped two miles from Round Rock, on the International and Great Northern Railway. After reconnoitering, it was determined to rob the bank in the town after resting the horses. Preparations were made for the descent on the moneybags. Bass was to go in, and Barnes was to hand a bill to the cashier to change. While doing so the chief was to present a six-shooter to his head, and order him to throw up his hands. Barnes was then to jump over the counter, enter the safe, and fill up his bag with money, while Jackson and Murphy were to stand in the doors and prevent persons from coming in during the process.

"In the meantime, and whilst the state authorities were kept informed by Murphy, the latter pretended his horse was broken down, and had to be rested, his object being to stave off the descent on the bank long enough for the arrival of the Rangers and his men. Bass determined to make the descent on Saturday, the 19th of July. After the robbery the chief and his bandits were to escape to the forests to the northward of the town.

"On Friday, the day before the projected robbery, Bass, Jackson and Barnes went into the town, hitching their horses in the suburbs, their purpose being to make a more thorough examination of the bank, take notes, and map out the general surroundings. With their old, slouched hats and saddlebags on their arms, they, of course, easily passed among the villagers for plain, simple country farmers. Then these pretended boobies from the rural districts quietly walked into a store of general merchandise, kept by a man named Koppel. They asked for plug tobacco. Koppel himself was sitting outside the store on the sidewalk enjoying the cool summer breeze, it being about midday. His young clerk, a man named Jude, waited on the farmers, and showed Bass several brands of the best tobacco he had. They were just about agreeing on the price.

"Town Deputy Sheriff Grimes then wandered in to look around. Thinking the tall farmer who did the trading seemed a bit shady, and seeing under his coat, not knowing the desperado, stepped up and asked him if he had a pistol, with the purpose of arresting him for violation of a state law. Bass answered, 'Yes,' and instantly the three robbers drew their pistols and began firing on the officer, who staggered out on the sidewalk, and falling, immediately expired. 'Hold up, boys!' was his only and last exclamation.

"Major Jones raced onto the action. One of the robbers leveled his six-shooter at his head and deliberately fired, the ball missing its aim but a few inches. Barnes was shot through the head and fell dead. Murphy, the spy, fortunately for himself was not with the robbers in the fight."[47]

Sam Bass was shot while trying to jump on his horse and escape. He had just climbed into his saddle when the fatal shot from one of the Texas posse found him. Stunned, Bass sat completely still for a moment. He looked pale and sick, and his hand was bleeding as he slowly attempted to load his gun. He managed to turn his horse away from the action and spurred him into a run. Bass was struggling to stay in the saddle as his ride carried him quickly out of town.[48]

The posses responsible for pursuing Sam Bass and his gang and shooting it out with the outlaws in Round Rock, Texas, followed after Sam, but it was getting dark, and they lost his trail. The lawmen resumed their search the following morning. They found Bass lying under a tree near an open prairie by the railroad tracks. He was near death and writhing in pain.[49]

A physician from Round Rock was summoned to the wounded outlaw. The doctor pronounced the wounds to be fatal and informed the bandit his last hours were close at hand. Bass was transported into town and placed on a cot in a windowless, plank house. His body was riddled with bullets, the fatal one having entered the small of his back and passing through to the front.[50]

Major Jones and Captain Peak tried to get Bass to make a statement about his illegal activities. "Bass, you have done much wrong in this world," Major Jones told the dying man, according to Sam Bass's biography. "You now have an opportunity to do some good before you die by giving some information which will lead to the vindication of that justice which you have so often defied and the law which you have constantly violated."

"No, I won't tell," Bass replied.

"Why won't you?" Major Jones queried.

"Because it is agin [*sic*] my profession to blow on my pals. If a man knows anything he ought to die it with him," Bass explained.[51]

The statements he did decide to make were well-known facts about individuals beyond the reach of future justice. Among these statements, he said: "I am twenty-seven years old, have brothers John and Denton, at

Mitchell, Indiana. Have been in the robbing business a long time. Had done much business of that kind before the U. P. robbery last fall."[52]

The interrogation continued:

Q.—How come you commenced this kind of life?

A.—Started out sporting on horse.

Q.—Why did you get worse than horse racing?

A.—Because they robbed me of my first $300.

Q.—After they robbed you, what did you do next?

A.—Went to robbing stages in the Black Hills—robbed seven. Got very little money. Jack Davis, Nixon, and myself were all that were in the Black Hills stage robberies. Joel Collins, Bill Heffridge, Tom Nixon, Jack Davis, Jim Berry, and me were in the Union Pacific robbery. Tom Nixon is in Canada. Have not seen him since that robbery. Jack Davis was in New Orleans from the time of the Union Pacific robbery till he went to Denton to get me to go in with him and buy a ship. This was the last of April, 1878. Gardner, living in Atascosa County, is my friend. Was at his house last fall. Went to Kansas with him once. Will not tell who was in the Eagle Ford robbery beside myself and Barnes. When we were in the store at Round Rock, Grimes asked me if I had a pistol, I said yes; then all three of us drew our pistols and shot him. If I killed Grimes it was the first man I ever killed. Henry Collins was with me in Salt Creek fight four or five weeks ago. Arkansas Johnson was killed in that fight. Don't know whether Underwood was wounded or not at Salt Creek fight. "Sebe" Barnes, Frank Jackson, and Charles Carter were there. We were all set afoot in that fight, but stole horses enough to remount ourselves in three hours, or as soon as dark came; after which we went back to Denton. Stayed there until we came to Round Rock.

Q.—Where is Jackson now?

A.—I don't know.

Q.—How do you usually meet after being scattered?

A.—Generally told by a friend.

Q.—Who are these friends?

A.—I will not tell.

"This was his usual reply to questions which he did not wish to answer, and was in the most deliberate manner possible.

"Even in the midst of his intense agony on Sunday afternoon he clung to the delusion that he would recover. But about twenty minutes before his death, when warned by his physician that dissolution was near at hand, he calmly replied, 'Let me go.'

"A few minutes later he said to his nurse, 'The world is bobbing around me.' His pain had ceased and he rested at ease. There were a few gasps and he was dead. This was at 4 p.m., Sunday, June 21."[53]

Sam Bass was buried the following morning. His body was interred at Round Rock.[54]

Captain Peak and his accomplished posse were given credit for helping to bring Sam Bass to justice. They were successful in driving Sam Bass from north Texas toward his ultimate capture and death in Round Rock. Chasing Bass all the way to Round Rock was something for which the laws of the state made no monetary provisions once the search had gone on for more than sixty days. The search for Bass officially began in late September 1877. The outlaw was caught nine months later. Captain Peak and his men would have followed Bass to the end without being paid; nothing stood in the way of bringing outlaws to justice, not even money.[55]

MANAGEMENT PRINCIPLES LEARNED FROM THE POSSE AFTER BRONCO BILL WALTERS

COMMIT TO FOCUSED DISCIPLINE.

True discipline is about making yourself emotionally commit time and effort regardless of external factors. Officer Jeff Milton and the posse after Bronco Bill Walters recognized this as they rode through a torrential downpour in Granite Pass, New Mexico. Regardless of the weather, they pulled their slickers around their necks and pressed on through the storm. Bronco Bill had to be stopped, and nothing would stand in the way.

STAND UP FOR WHAT YOU BELIEVE IN, EVEN IF YOU'RE STANDING ALONE.

Jeff Milton wanted to make sure Bronco Bill answered for robbing trains. He asked for a leave of absence from his job as a Wells Fargo messenger to pursue the outlaw, but his request was denied. Milton threatened to resign his post in order to chase the thief, and the company executives changed their minds. Only after he stood up for what he believed was right did everything work out satisfactorily.

DON'T WAIT FOR THE STORM TO PASS BEFORE YOU TAKE ACTION.

Tracking outlaws through the White Mountains was treacherous, but waiting for the possibility that the criminals would break through to open land and escape was not an option. The posse had to pursue the bandits through harsh country or risk losing the desperadoes' trail. What had to be done had to be done right then.

NEVER DODGE THE DIFFICULTIES.

All problems become smaller if you don't dodge them, but confront them. Milton and his posse decided to face Bronco Bill with their guns drawn. Bill drew his weapon in response and began firing at the lawmen. It would have been easy to flee the scene, but the posse chose instead to have it out with the desperado and end the pursuit once and for all.

FOCUS ON THE SKILLS YOU'VE GAINED.

Jeff Milton returned to his job as a Wells Fargo messenger after Bronco Bill was placed in jail. Milton had learned a great deal about train robbers from his time tracking the outlaw and employed what he'd learned at his job. He was always ready with a gun and kept a careful eye on the cargo he was entrusted to transport safely. What Milton learned while riding with the posse paved the way for a job with the Immigration Service.

CHAPTER SEVEN

Do What Has to Be Done: The Posse After Bronco Bill Walters

Five riders moved swiftly across the open country through Granite Pass in southwest New Mexico. An electrical storm lit up the sky around them, and a deluge of hail broke free from the clouds, pelting the men in their saddles and their horses. Sounding like a troop of demons advancing, the wind howled and screamed as it pushed over the massive walls of rock the riders passed.

Former peace officer Jefferson Davis Milton rode in front of the others. He was a tall man with sloping shoulders, his granitelike visage partly hidden by a dark mustache that curled around to meet his thick sideburns. George W. Scarborough, a blue-eyed, gruff-looking, onetime lawman from El Paso, Texas, took a position on Jeff's left. Eugene Thacker, the youthful son of a railroad detective, rode on Jeff's right side. Directly behind the three were Bill Martin and Thomas Bennett, Diamond A Ranch cowboys turned bounty hunters. The men pulled their slickers around their necks and urged their mounts on through the tempest. Claps of thunder ushered in another downpour of hail.[1]

The determined riders, members of a posse pursuing a gang of train-robbing outlaws, were soaked to the bone once they reached Fort Apache, a military post near Coolidge Lake. No one said a word as they made camp outside the garrison's gates. Discussing the obstacles on the way toward achieving that goal wasn't necessary. Their focus was on capturing Bronco Bill Walters and his boys.[2]

William E. Walters, also known as Bronco Bill Walters, was from Fort Sill, Oklahoma. What he did before being hired at the Diamond A Ranch in 1889 is anyone's guess. It's what he did after getting a job as a cowhand that warranted attention. The Diamond A was a five-hundred-square-mile spread nestled in the boot heel of New Mexico. The magnificent acres of grass there made it the perfect spot for raising cattle. The ranch was always in need of workers. Cowpunchers that dropped by looking for employment were generally hired on the spot. It was considered a rude violation of the proprieties of a cow camp to inquire into a man's connections or character. Just wanting to work was enough. Bronco Bill Walters wanted to work, and that's all that mattered and all the foreman at the Diamond A would have cared about if Bronco Bill hadn't desired more than the job had to offer.[3]

During long, dull evenings around the campfire, Bronco Bill contemplated a life that was exciting and profitable. He thought about robbing a stage or a train. He imagined how he would tackle such a daring feat and rehearsed a getaway. After a while, it wasn't enough only to imagine such actions. Bronco Bill left the Diamond A Ranch in the fall of 1890 in search of excitement and money.[4]

In mid-October of 1890, Bronco Bill and an associate named Mike McGinnis rode into the town of Hachita, New Mexico. The small community was bustling with railroad workers, cattle drovers, and copper miners. One evening at the saloon, Walters and McGinnis made the acquaintance of a prospector named Jackson. Sometime during their brief encounter, they learned that the miner would be leaving town soon, carrying more than $430 with him. The would-be thieves planned to follow Jackson and, when the time was right, take his money.[5]

Bronco Bill and his cohort trailed Jackson to Separ, New Mexico, where the miner checked into a hotel. The bandits did the same. The pair then hatched a scheme they believed would drive all the customers from the establishment, leaving their possessions behind. Walters and McGinnis sat in their room drinking until late in the evening. When all was quiet, the two raced out into the lobby and began firing their pistols in the air. The noise rudely awakened the hotel patrons with a start. They all fled the business in fear of being shot. Bronco Bill and McGinnis seized the moment, ran to Jackson's room, and began the search for his money. It was nowhere to be found. The panicked prospector had taken the cash with him when he'd hurried out of the building.[6]

The thwarted thieves were furious that their crime had not gone off as planned. Feeling no pain, Bronco Bill and McGinnis decided to take their frustrations out on Separ. The men ran throughout the town shooting at anything that didn't move. A telegraph message was sent out to county sheriff Harvey Whitehill, who was away on business in Lordsburg. As the night progressed, the unsuccessful bandits decided to go to bed and sleep off the effects of the alcohol and the agony of a failed robbery.[7]

The following day when Sheriff Whitehill arrived on the scene, he and his deputies marched to the hotel, roused Bronco Bill and McGinnis out of their beds, and hauled them to jail. The men remained in jail until February 16, 1891, when they escaped confinement and fled the area. The law hunted the escapees down, and when Bronco Bill was recaptured in late May 1891, he was escorted back to jail. After a quick hearing, Walters was sentenced to a year in prison.[8]

Bronco Bill was a model prisoner and earned early release for his exemplary behavior. When the prison cell was opened on April 13, 1892, the cowhand, turned bandit and convict, returned to the Diamond A. He was immediately hired back, still with no questions asked,

COURTESY OF THE STATE ARCHIVES OF NEW MEXICO

William Walters, aka Bronco Bill.

and for the next three years was content to work tending to the livestock. In 1895, Bronco Bill abandoned the straight-and-narrow path
again and returned to his former calling, that of outlaw.[9]

With no real plan for the future, Bronco Bill drifted from mining
town to mining town in southwestern New Mexico. During a brief
stay in Cooney, New Mexico, he broke into a saloon and relieved the
owner of a couple of weapons and less than two dollars in cash. After
learning who the culprit was, the authorities tracked Bronco Bill to
Silver City and arrested him for the crime. While awaiting trial at the
Socorro County jail, Bill and nine other felons escaped. Bronco Bill
made his getaway on a stolen horse. After days on the run, he wandered

into Deming, New Mexico. There he made the acquaintance of a young woman who found something endearing about the fugitive and decided to let him hide out at her place. The authorities eventually caught up with Bill, but he refused to surrender his weapon and go peacefully back to jail. Shots were exchanged, and once more Bronco Bill managed to flee the scene.[10]

The escaped bandit's next stop was Israel King's X Ranch in Chihuahua, Mexico. The working ranch was a refuge for many felons. Bronco Bill was safe for a short time, but when law enforcement agents infiltrated the sanctuary in search of cattle that had been rustled, the desperado was once again on the run. Bronco Bill traveled to El Paso, Texas. In mid-May 1896, he was enjoying a beer at the Senate Saloon when the local sheriff confronted him about his horse tied in front. A warrant had been issued for Bill Walters's arrest on the charge of stealing a horse from the property owner in Deming. A newspaper article about Bronco Bill's run-in with the law was seen by authorities in Socorro County, New Mexico. They quickly had the governor of New Mexico petition the governor of Texas to have Bill transferred to New Mexico. All was agreed on, and an agent was dispatched to El Paso to escort the prisoner back to the place where he had perpetrated one of his first crimes.[11]

By late June 1896, Bronco Bill was locked tightly in a cell in Socorro County. When the outlaw was brought before the judge in November 1896, he pled guilty to robbing the saloon in Cooney, but the matter of stealing a horse was oddly enough never heard. What was discussed was the medical evaluation of the prisoner by the county physician. The doctor reported that Bronco Bill was in poor health, and if he remained behind bars, he would die. The judge was moved by the doctor's assessment of the inmate and ordered Bill's release.[12]

Within an hour after being released from jail in Socorro County, Bill was rearrested and taken to Deming to appear before a judge there.

He would have to answer for shooting at the sheriff and his deputies. A fast-talking lawyer helped Bronco Bill avoid long-term confinement. Once again the bandit was allowed to go free. The close calls he had with the law were not enough to reform him, however. His crimes accumulated throughout 1897 and 1898. As his daring acts of thievery continued, he was joined by other lawbreakers with the same drive to take what wasn't theirs.[13]

Bronco Bill was associated most closely with fellow outlaw William "Kid" Johnson. On March 29, 1898, the pair decided to rob the Santa Fe Pacific, a passenger train headed west. The vehicle had just come to a stop at the station in Grants, New Mexico, when the daring outlaws attempted their act just after midnight. Both Bronco Bill and Bill Johnson approached the train with their guns drawn. One of them opened fire, and the conductor, Charles Berry, who was on the platform, ran around the depot in order to escape the flying bullets. The express messenger and special guard on the train opened the door of the express car when they heard shots fired. Realizing quickly that the train was being robbed, they began firing back at the robbers.[14]

"One of the robbers, who had taken his position in front, shot out the headlights of the engine, and ordered the engineer workman to pull up the train, to point where, no doubt, they intended to blow open the express car," the March 29, 1898, edition of the *Albuquerque Citizen* reported. "The engineer complied with the robber's positive request, leaving the conductor at the depot, but after running the train a few hundred yards the engineer backed back to the depot. The robbers in the meantime had realized their failure and had decamped in the direction of the lava beds, and it is almost positive that they carried away with them one of their number who was evidently hit by a bullet from either the express messenger or guard.

"After the fusillade of shots, the conductor wired the facts to Train-master Allen at Gallup, who transmitted the information forthwith to Superintendent Wells and Division Superintendent Hibbard.

"Acting on advice, Trainmaster Allen conducted together a posse of men, well-armed, at Gallup, and at daylight this morning they were in the saddle and in pursuit of the robbers.

"On a special train from here this morning was Fred Fornoff, who joined the posse organized at Grants at one o'clock this morning, and with two posses in the field it is hoped the robbers will be captured.

"A short time ago the saloon of Kitchen and Kennedy at Gallup was held up and robbed in broad daylight, and it is thought by the mar-shal of that town that the perpetrators of last night's attempted train robbery were the same persons."[15]

The failed holdup left one railroad employee wounded and Bronco Bill and Bill Johnson racing toward the White Mountains, with two posses chasing after them. The outlaws lost the men in pursuit of them in the Double Circle mountain range near Ruidoso. The bandits pushed on until they reached the Double Circle Ranch on Eagle Creek. While they were there, the duo met another criminal wanting to join forces with them. James "Jim" Burnett was an overly confident man who talked too much. The boys killed Burnett while on the trail. A chance encounter with the law near the White Mountains led both Bronco Bill and Bill Johnson to believe that Burnett had been working with authorities to capture them.[16]

On May 26, 1898, Walters and Johnson robbed a mail train near Belen, New Mexico. The thieves stole $20,000 from a Wells Fargo safe on board. The pair headed west into the mountains while Undersheriff F. X. Vigil of Los Lunas gathered a posse which consisted of his dep-uty, Dan Bustamante, several Indians, and aides. It wasn't long before Sheriff Vigil's posse had picked up the outlaws' trail and was closing in.

The posse overtook the train robbers at Angelito Ranch, sixty-five miles west of Belen.[17]

The robbers were preparing to leave camp when Sheriff Vigil ordered the posse to circle around behind them. Vigil and Deputy Bustamante closed in on the outlaws from the opposite side. The robbers were in the act of saddling their rides when Sheriff Vigil, at a distance of one hundred feet, suddenly appeared and demanded their surrender.[18]

"A general fusillade of firing immediately began," a report in the *Albuquerque Citizen* from May 26, 1898, read. "Sheriff Vigil, Deputy Bustamante, and an Indian tracker were killed. One of the robbers is believed to have been fatally wounded. They fled on foot to the mountains. The remaining Indians with the posse captured the outlaws' horses."[19]

Bill Johnson had been shot in the neck, and Bronco Bill caught bullets in the hip and shoulder. The men buried the money they'd stolen, then dragged their tired and bloody bodies to the W Slash Ranch. Someone at the ranch dressed their wounds, and the outlaws hurried on their way, riding a pair of borrowed horses. They put up at the Double Circle Ranch again. Bronco Bill sent a cowhand into town to Fort Apache for drugs to care for the injuries. Once the desperadoes were well, they returned for their money and proceeded on their way toward Arizona.[20]

Jeff Milton and his posse were well aware of the deeds Bronco Bill and Bill Johnson had done. Their exploits had been well publicized. Warrants for their arrest had been issued and rewards were being offered for their apprehension. Both Jeff Milton and George Scarborough had reputations for being tough and tenacious. They were veterans of numerous gun battles and had engaged in disputes with some of the West's most deadly outlaws, including John Wesley Hardin.[21]

Milton was working as a Wells Fargo express messenger on the Southern Pacific that traveled from Benson, Arizona, to Guaymas, Mexico, when he got word of Bronco Bill and Bill Johnson's crime spree. Milton was determined to run the robbers down and asked Wells Fargo executives for a leave of absence. His request was denied, so he then threatened to resign. Wells Fargo executives quickly changed their minds. The division manager was pleased to know someone with Milton's background was going to track the outlaws who were terrorizing the line. He furnished a car for Milton to travel in and one for his horse. Milton sent a wire to George Scarborough, Bill Martin, and Eugene Thacker, asking them to accompany him on the ride. Milton boarded a train in Tucson, Arizona, bound for New Mexico. The car was filled with all the provisions needed to sustain him and his posse on the hunt for Bronco Bill and Bill Johnson.[22]

While en route to meet Scarborough, Martin, and Thacker in Deming, Milton learned that the desperadoes were planning a holdup around Holbrook, Arizona. The men would ride the rails through the area, hoping the thieves would try to rob the train they were on.[23]

Bronco Bill and Bill Johnson were in Arizona, but they had no plans to rob a train. The outlaws had recruited another bandit, Daniel "Red" Pipkin, and the three wanted to socialize before embarking on any other crime. They rode into Geronimo, Arizona, bought themselves new suits of clothes, treated themselves to shaves, haircuts, and baths, and invited themselves to a Fourth of July dance at the schoolhouse in town.[24]

A report of the incident in the July 25, 1898, edition of the *Arizona Republic* noted that the dance was already in progress when the criminals stepped into the doorway holding their guns in their hands. Bronco Bill announced to the fearful onlookers that they didn't want any trouble, they'd just come to dance. Johnson and Pipkin kept their guns leveled at the crowd while Bronco Bill eyed the ladies sitting with their escorts. He holstered his gun and asked one of the women for a dance. She turned him down, so he went to the next. One by one all refused to dance with him.[25]

Bronco Bill was offended by the behavior of the women and let his irritation over their bad manners be known by drawing his weapon and shooting at the ladies' feet. Johnson and Pipkin joined in the shooting, too, firing at the lights. The guests scattered frantically, trying to get out of the building. Many burst through the glass windows and dove through the frames into the night. The rowdy outlaws eventually made a hasty departure.[26]

News of what occurred at the Independence Day dance in Geronimo was covered in newspapers throughout the Southwest. Milton received a wire letting him know that the three bandits had been identified as the ones he was trying to lure into a train robbery. He quickly ordered the train to take him and the posse to Geronimo. When Milton and his men arrived, they jumped their horses out of the car and hurried to question the townspeople who had witnessed the mayhem. Milton was told the bandits were headed northeast in the direction of Fort Apache, Arizona.[27]

The bounty hunters braved a fierce rainstorm following after the outlaws. They stopped briefly at Fort Apache for supplies, then resumed their search for the criminals.[28]

For several days they hunted for Bronco Bill through the torturous intricacies of torn terrain that made up the White Mountains. The posse rode through miles of dense forests and trekked over rocky streams, encountering inclement weather and harsh winds before coming across a clue that assured them they were on the right path. On a trail above the timberline, the men found a tin can with the Diamond A brand scratched on it. They were certain Bronco Bill and his followers had passed that way.[29]

The posse continued until they reached a clearing that included a pen made of pine logs. Cowhands at the Double Circle Ranch occasionally used the pen to corral stray horses. Milton thought the spot

COURTESY OF THE ARIZONA HISTORICAL SOCIETY

Sheriff Jefferson Davis Milton.

looked like a place outlaws might take refuge. He decided the posse should hide in the thick trees around the perimeter of the crude corral and wait to see if Bronco Bill showed. On the second day of the watch, a cowpuncher drove a handful of horses into the pen. Drawing his six-gun, Milton greeted the unsuspecting man, named John Gibson, with an order to put up his hands. Gibson complied. John informed Milton that he was not part of Bronco Bill's group, but admitted to knowing where they were. The bandits were at the Double Crossing horse camp near an area called McBride Crossing. John offered to lead the posse to the outlaws. Milton and his men agreed.[30]

On Friday, July 29, 1898, Milton and his posse overtook the horse camp where John Gibson led them. They apprehended eight cowpunchers, but Bronco Bill, Johnson, and Pipkin were nowhere to be seen. The Double Circle crew under guard wanted to admit openly they knew where the desperadoes had gone. Privately, Milton learned the three outlaws were due to return to camp the following morning.[31]

According to George Scarborough's account of the arrest of Bronco Bill, found in the August 29, 1898, edition of the *Los Angeles Herald*, the posse spotted the lawbreakers riding toward the camp at nine o'clock on Saturday morning. Milton and Scarborough watched the bandits approach from behind a copse of trees. Halfway to the camp, two of the men stopped and shot at a rattlesnake that was under a large rock. The third man continued on. The closer he got to them, the more it became clear to the posse that the rider was Bronco Bill. Bill climbed off his horse once he had reached the camp, but stopped to look around before going any further. He sensed something wasn't right, and just as he was about to swing back into the saddle, Milton stepped from behind the trees with a shotgun leveled at the fugitive.[32]

"Hold on there, Cap," Milton said in a natural tone of voice. "I want to speak to you."[33]

In a split second, Bill had his six-shooter spitting fire, his arm extended. Milton shot back. His bullet hit Bronco Bill in his elbow, shattering the bone. The bullet passed through his chest and lodged on the other side, under his left arm. Bill fell to the ground, and his horse trotted away from him.[34]

"About this time we were conscious that somebody else was in the fight," Scarborough told the *Los Angeles Herald* newspaper reporter. "A bullet sung by my ear and tore up the earth a short distance behind me. Johnson and Pipkin, who were still on the hill when the firing commenced below, had taken shelter behind a large rock and were firing at us. I could just see their hat brims. They were about four hundred yards from us at that time.

"We commenced a bombardment of the rock and made it so hot for them that they ran. As they came from behind the rock we shot both horses, when Johnson took refuge behind a large juniper tree close by and returned the fire. All that I could see was his hips. I took a dead rest and fired, and Johnson fell over and commenced to yell like a panther. I knew that he was bad hit. Pipkin fled over the hill and we never saw him again. We went up to Johnson and found that he was shot through the hip and was suffering great agony. We carried him down to camp and laid him beside Bronco Bill, who had just regained consciousness.

"The fight was over. We had expected to stay in that country for three months if necessary, but in less than three weeks we had captured our men.

"After the excitement had subsided a man was sent to Fort Apache for a doctor, and also one to Clifton. Sunday Deputy Sheriffs Simpson of Geronimo and Clark of Clifton arrived on the ground and accompanied the posse to Geronimo, where they arrived Wednesday afternoon. Johnson died at the horse camp late Sunday night. Before his death his yells could be heard for two miles. His agony was something terrible to witness, and without medical assistance the posse was unable to give him any relief. Before he died he was asked if he had any word to send his aged father. He was propped up in bed and with great difficulty sent the following message to his father, who lived on Blue River about forty miles from the scene of the killing. Slowly the words came from those lips now growing ice cold in death. The men stood around in silence with uncovered heads and the moon shone faintly through the trees and lighted up the camp with its friendly beams: 'Tell Father,' he said, 'not to grieve after me. I brought it all on myself. Tell him not to hold anyone responsible for my death.' Here he was seized with paroxysms of pain. His features were convulsed and his cries made a man's blood turn cold. With a last effort he continued, 'Just tell him, boys, that Bill said good-bye.'

"He never said another word. His eyes were closed in that eternal sleep from which there is no awakening in this world.

"Bill and Johnson said only a few words to each other after they were shot, although they lay side by side on the same cot for an entire day.

"Monday morning the start was made for Geronimo with 'Bronco Bill.' An improvised bed was arranged on a pack horse, and he was laid on it as gently as possible and the start was made for Geronimo, fifty miles away.

"Bronco Bill stood the pain as long as possible, and then in those quiet even tones without a tremor he said: 'Boys, just throw this pack outfit over the hill and saddle me a horse, and I'll lead the way into town.' This was done, and Bill led the procession, and what nerve! Although suffering great pain every step he laughed and joked with the posse, telling of numerous little scrapes in which he had played the leading part. Whistling and laughing, and shot through and through, he went to meet his fate as if it was a picnic excursion.

"During the ride to Bowie he made frequent calls for 'the bottle'; he never entered into any conversation. He ate peaches and smoked a cigar and seemed determined to make himself as comfortable as possible.

"At Bowie he was hustled across the platform and into the hotel, where he was soon in bed, and shortly afterwards partook of a light supper. Afterwards as he lay on the bed surrounded by several of the posse, he told the following story.

"'My true name is William Walters, and I will be twenty-nine years old next October. I have been a cowboy for the past twelve years, and have traveled over a great part of Arizona, Texas, New Mexico, and Old Mexico. I have had some pretty scary times in those twelve years, but boys,' he said, and he opened his eyes and looked us square in the eyes, 'there is no man that can say that I ever murdered anybody. These marks on my neck and shoulder will show that. When I rode into that horse camp last Saturday morning, I knew the game had come to a showdown. I knew there was no escape left for me, but I thought if I made the fight, the other boys might be able to drag it. I opened the ball, boys, and you know the rest.'"[35]

A *Los Angeles Herald* reporter asked: "Mr. Walters, do you deny these charges that are made against you?"[36]

"Bill opened his eyes about halfway and drawled: 'Well, by gawd, young feller, if you'll please tell Bill what he is charged with, he might answer that question for you.'

"He slept tolerably easy the rest of the night, and the next morning at daybreak found him seated in the dining room eating his breakfast. Afterwards he strolled up and down the platform by himself with that large black hat pulled over his eyes. He looked pale and weak and swayed slightly as he walked. The train came from the west and they loaded him on. He sat in the day coach and as the train left, he smiled through the window and waved his hand to the small crowd of onlookers at the depot."[37]

Bronco Bill eventually recovered from his wounds, stood trial, and was sentenced for life to the penitentiary at Santa Fe. He was pardoned after twenty years and returned to work on the Diamond A Ranch.[38]

Jeff Milton let his posse go and returned to his job with Wells Fargo. He thwarted robberies of the express cars he guarded and survived a serious bullet wound to his left upper arm. In 1904, he took a job in Tucson with the Immigration Service—a forerunner of the Border Patrol—as a mounted inspector, trying to restrict the flow of illegal Chinese immigration. Milton retired in 1932 at the age of seventy. Known as the first border patrolman, he died at his home in Tucson, Arizona, on May 7, 1947. He was eighty-five years old.[39]

Management Principles Learned from the Posse after Juan Soto

Analyze Your Adversaries.

To be successful, you can't be afraid to study and learn about your adversaries—their strengths, weaknesses, and their allies. Sheriff Harry Morse found out all he could about Juan Soto and the men who followed him. Knowing the outlaw's habits, previous criminal histories, and known associates helped aid the posse in their search for the criminal. Once you have made a careful decision based on facts, go into action.

Know When It's Time to Retrace Your Steps.

Law enforcement agents use this procedure to find out what happened at a crime scene. It can help determine where one might have gotten off course and just what needs to be reset in order to ensure positive results. Sheriff Morse and his men reexamined the scene of Soto's crime in Sunol in order to find something they might have missed the first time. The process led them to question ranchers in the vicinity who helped the bandit get away.

Negotiate the Best Deal.

Negotiation is a big part of life. Knowing how to negotiate effectively in both competitive and collaborative situations is essential to achieving a mutually beneficial outcome. When Sheriff Morse and the posse happened on a sheepherder afraid to share when he knew about Juan Soto, it was imperative for the lawman to work out a deal that would help the witness feel safe and get the information they needed about where the bandit was located.

Accept Success with Humility and Gratitude.

Sheriff Harry Morse's duel to the death with Juan Soto remains California's most famous outlaw–lawman gunfight. After his successful quest to stop Soto, the community at large was so impressed with Morse's work that they suggested he run for political office. The lawman declined the invitation. He was grateful for the vote of confidence, but believed his talent was in law enforcement. He politely thanked his supporters and went back to the job of fighting crime.

CHAPTER EIGHT

ACCEPT SUCCESS WITH HUMILITY AND GRATITUDE: THE POSSE AFTER JUAN SOTO

Sheriff Harry Morse removed a Model 1866 Winchester carbine rifle from the leather holster on his saddle and cocked it to make sure he had a bullet in the chamber. He surveyed the sprawling canyon deep in the depth of the Panoche Hills, more than fifty miles outside of Gilroy, California. In the distance below were three small adobe houses, and Morse had every reason to suspect members of outlaw Juan Soto's gang were inside one of the buildings.[1]

High above the sheriff and his eight-member posse was a seem-ingly inexhaustible mat of black, rainless clouds moving steadily across the world. Morse watched the sun disappear behind the billows and exchanged a determined look with Captain Theodore Winchell, on horseback next to him. Winchell, an undersheriff from Alameda County, had been riding with Sheriff Morse for several months in search of the fugitive. San Jose sheriff Nick Harris and six other deputies made up the rest of the posse. All of the lawmen had years of experience track-ing lawbreakers through the Northern California terrain. Each was an exceptional shot and could hold his own in hand-to-hand combat.[2]

Harry Morse had been sheriff of Alameda County for more than seven years. From 1864, when he took the job, to April 1871, when he peered down on the possible hiding place of Juan Soto's men, Morse had traversed the hills and plains of eastern and northern Alameda County in search of horse thieves, highwaymen, and cutthroats. Until Morse took the job at twenty-eight years of age, most lawmen had been too afraid to venture very far to catch outlaws, worried they would be outnumbered. Thus, the criminals were able to go about their business, relatively unconcerned about being apprehended. Sheriff Morse, along with Nick Harris and Theodore Winchell, changed all that.[3]

The officers and their deputies familiarized themselves with the haunts of the outlaws and the topography of the country where the bad guys were known to roam. They learned the locations of ranches, springs, and mountain trails, as well as acquainting themselves with the inhabitants and their occupations. They knew where to hide and wait along trails for lawbreakers to pass, and armed with that knowledge, they knew what to do to avoid an ambush.[4]

Juan Soto, the man Sheriff Morse and his posse were tracking, was a thief and a murderer. He had a reputation as a brutal man who would stop at nothing to get what he wanted. Soto mainly operated in the central part of California, but, like the other bandits before him, went wherever the possibility of loot beckoned. For more than four years, the six-foot-two, 220-pound, half-Indian, half-Mexican man had terrorized the area from the Livermore Valley to San Luis Obispo. Soto and his gang of desperadoes robbed stages, stage stops, lone emigrants, and prospectors. Their victims were often beaten or killed. Soto's dark features and general expression of animal ferocity earned him the name "the human wildcat." He had black, slightly crossed eyes, a mane of black hair, and a bushy beard and mustache. The April 10, 1871, edition of the *San Francisco Chronicle* described his appearance as the "physical manifestation of as cruel a spirit as ever animated a human being."[5]

The activities of Soto, and those like him, are best illustrated in the following figures posted in the July 12, 1925, edition of the *Los Angeles*

COURTESY OF JOHN BOESSENECKER

Illustration of Sheriff Harry Morse's encounter with the notorious outlaw, Juan Soto.

Times. "From 1849 to 1854," the newspaper article noted, "[a period of] five years . . . 4,200 persons were murdered in California. In 1855, 588 met death by violence, and 47 were reported executed by mobs.

"It was unsafe to travel alone in any part of California south of Alameda County, either near the coast or the interior. Small groups of miners suspected of having made a stake were pounced upon and killed, shot or ambushed as they labored over their pans in the streams. Peace officers were either in league with the bandits or cowed by them so that they winked at murderers."[6]

Convinced that there was no one in law enforcement who would ever challenge him or attempt to capture him, Soto rested comfortably in hideouts scattered throughout the area. Surrounded by gang members and their paramours, he planned their next criminal acts in between hands of poker. Like the famous outlaw who mentored him, Tiburcio Vasquez, Soto believed the crimes he perpetrated on newer settlers were justified. American pioneers were viewed by many California natives as people who would remove any obstacle to take over and settle the land.[7]

Soto hated the Americans who were slowly establishing law and order in the territory. On January 10, 1871, Soto and his gang planned and executed a crime they believed would demonstrate the depth of their resentment toward the determined settlers they referred to as "piggish gringos."[8]

A Sunol store clerk, known throughout the tiny village in Alameda County as Otto Ludovici, tidied the shelves and swept the floor of the business after a long day's work. The store owner's wife, Mrs. Thomas Scott, and her three children were assisting in the routine of closing the business by refilling candy jars, folding bolts of fabric, and restacking blankets. Otto weaved past his helpers, walked over to the door, and locked it. As he turned the key, a large rock shattered the front window. The door suddenly flew open, and Juan Soto and several of his rough associates stepped inside.[9]

Mrs. Scott gathered her terrified children close to her. Otto slowly backed away from the bandits, unsure of what to do next. "I'm afraid we're closed now," the petrified clerk stammered. "We'll open again in the morning." Soto laughed a little at how frightened the man appeared. "I don't plan to buy anything, *señor* . . . today or tomorrow," the desperado said coldly. "But take . . . that I will do."[10]

Otto cast a glance at a rifle on the counter next to him, but before he could make a move, Soto pulled out his six-gun and shot the clerk in the chest. The man fell to the floor in a heap.

Mrs. Scott hurried her children out of the room and down the hall, quickly disappearing with them into a storage area. A sly smile of content spread across Soto's face as he watched them flee. While his outlaw group looted the store, Soto cocked his gun and fired several volleys in the direction of the place where Mrs. Scott and her brood were hiding. Their screams filled the air and they could be heard crying. Soto then reloaded his weapon and assisted the bandits in looting the store.[11]

The crooks were so preoccupied with the robbery that they didn't notice Mrs. Scott running out the back door with her youngsters in tow. Soto looked up just in time to see them scurry across the street into a neighbor's house. Before he and his men fled the shop unopposed, Soto kicked the dead clerk in the side and cursed the deceased for his "unfortunate circumstances." Carrying $65 and a bundle of clothes in his arms, Soto ran away from the scene.[12]

The desperado's barbaric and depraved behavior incensed the residents in town and sent waves of terror washing over the outlying areas.

Law-abiding citizens may have been terrified of Soto, calling him "the most fearsome figure of an outlaw that ever roamed," but Harry Morse, Alameda County's tough, no-nonsense sheriff, vowed to go to the ends of the earth to "track Soto down and see that his head was placed in a noose." Morse was known as a persistent man hunter, having brought several noted California criminals like Norrato Ponee and Tiburcio Vasquez to justice. He was no less determined to capture Soto.[13]

Sheriff Morse and his men arrived on the scene of the murder of Otto Ludovici the day after the crime was committed. The intrepid lawman and his posse trailed Soto and his gang southward. They spent four days traversing the Santa Clara Valley, but to no avail. Soto had slipped away and was in hiding somewhere. Morse and his deputies returned to the store in Sunol where the brutal killing had taken place. The lawman wanted to retrace Soto's steps. The search began again, and this time Sheriff Morse decided to question ranchers. During a conversation with a rancher near Milpitas, the posse came across the bundle of clothes stolen from the mercantile. The residents at the property told authorities they had found the clothing behind the house. Morse didn't believe them and escorted them to the Alameda County jail. It was only when the rancher believed they could be incarcerated for theft that they admitted to having seen Soto and helping the bandit and his men get away. Soto gave the rancher and his family the clothes for their efforts.[14]

By early May 1871, Sheriff Morse, Captain Winchell, Sheriff Nick Harris, Deputy L. C. Morehouse of San Leandro, and six other lawmen resumed the search for Soto. The posse was working north through a narrow valley and had spent several days traveling over jumbled rocks. They had seen no signs of human life until they had encountered a sheepherder. Sheriff Morse approached the man to question him, but the man would barely respond. He leaned on his long staff and watched his flock indolently, shrugging at the queries or merely saying "*Quién sabe?*"[15]

Sheriff Morse didn't think the sheepherder was being honest. He noticed an uneasy flicker in the man's eyes when he mentioned Juan Soto's name. The lawman coolly climbed down off his horse, walked over to the sheepherder, jerked his gun from his holster, and thrust it into the man's ribs.[16]

"Listen, hombre," Morse announced, "we know that Juan Soto isn't far away. He came up this valley. You saw him, and you know where he is. Now tell me quick, or I'll kill you like a dog!"[17]

The sheepherder knew the lawman meant what he said. Trembling and ashen gray with fright, the man stammered. "Yes, *señor*, I do know where he is. But he is a terrible man! He cuts the hearts out of those who betray him. My own cousin he threatened so. I saw the body. So I dare not tell."[18]

"Juan Soto is all done," Sheriff Morse replied, placing his gun back in his holster. "He's killed his last man. You lead us to him. I'll take care of you."[19]

"Right up this canyon," the sheepherder explained. "It is perhaps eight or ten miles away. The place cannot be reached from above. That is why they have chosen it."[20]

One of the posse members offered the sheepherder a pack mule to ride. It was clear the posse wanted the man to lead the way. He reluctantly complied and, leaving his livestock behind, climbed aboard the mule and escorted the posse onward.[21]

The sheepherder led Sheriff Morse and his men to a ridge overlooking a secluded valley known as Sausalito. Immediately below them stood three adobe houses; the posse would have to pass by the buildings in order to get into the outlaw's stronghold a few miles farther up the canyon. Morse divided the posse into three parties, and each was assigned the duty of capturing one of the houses and securing the people found inside.[22]

Morse and Captain Winchell were to overtake the main house. They approached the building from the south and managed to reach the corral closest to it without being detected. A stable hand sauntered out of the corral carrying a bit and reins. He was preoccupied with inspecting the hardware in his hands and didn't notice the two constables at first. When the man finally did look up, he nodded to the lawmen as though their presence wasn't out of the ordinary. Pretending to be a pair of lost riders, Sheriff Morse quickly exchanged pleasantries with the worker and announced that he and his equally lost friend were thirsty and needed a drink.[23]

COURTESY OF JOHN BOESSENECKER

Juan Soto.

The stable hand nodded approvingly. The lawmen dismounted, and he led them to the main house. Sheriff Morse was carrying his revolver with him, and Captain Winchell was holding a double-barreled shotgun loaded with buckshot. The naive guide escorted the pair inside. The room was crowded with a dozen renegades, and among them was Juan Soto.[24]

Sheriff Morse and Soto locked eyes. Each recognized the other instantly. A long silence, heavy as doom, hung over the room. No one moved. A frieze of desperadoes stood at a bar, holding glasses of whiskey and waiting for the chance to drink the liquid down. Captain Winchell stood next to Morse—he swallowed hard; every nerve in his body on alert.[25]

Before any of Soto's men had a chance to assess the situation and react, Sheriff Morse jerked his gun from his holster and leveled it at the outlaw chief. He moved swiftly through the bandits until he was inches away from their leader. Soto carefully raised his hand and motioned for his men to hold their positions. He knew his men could take Morse in an ambush, but not before Morse killed him. Soto's men reluctantly did nothing.[26]

Sheriff Morse ordered Soto to "put up his hands." Soto sat sullenly gazing back at the officer, while a scowl of unutterable ugliness gathered about his shaggy brows and small bead-like eyes. Morse ordered him a second time to throw up his hands, threatening the desperado with instant death if the command were not obeyed. Soto didn't make a move; he simply continued his savage glare at the officer.[27]

Morse removed a pair of steel handcuffs from his belt and with his left hand passed them across his body to Captain Winchell, keeping the outlaw covered in the meantime with a pistol in his right.

"Put these on him, Winchell," he said.

Winchell took the bracelet, but made no motion toward the outlaw.

"Put them on him," Morse again ordered, growing angry at the lawman's hesitation. Winchell stood like he was dazed.

"Then cover him with your shotgun while I do it," Morse told Winchell. Morse was now keenly aware of the desperate job he had to do.[28]

Winchell cast a worried glance around the room. The lawmen were outnumbered. That thought had settled on Winchell, and he was scared beyond reason. He slowly backed out of the room, and when he reached the door, he turned and ran away. At almost the same moment, a fat woman standing near Morse lunged at him and grabbed his pistol arm. One of Soto's men jumped up and grabbed him from the other side.[29]

"*No tire en la casa!*" they both screamed as they threw themselves upon him. During the desperate struggle made by the deserted officer to free himself from the assailants, Soto sprang to his feet and stood behind one of his friends.[30]

Sheriff Morse managed to break free of the man and woman's grip. Soto's man ran toward the exit and raced out into the light. Morse raised his pistol over the person Soto was hiding behind and fired. The shot only knocked off Soto's hat. The miscue gave Soto a chance to reach for his gun. Morse jumped backwards through the open door before the outlaw could shoot. Soto followed behind him.[31]

Morse ran around to the open space behind the house and there turned to face his foe. Soto was furious, and his anger kept his aim from being true. He fired at Morse four times in quick succession, missing his target each time.[32]

Sheriff Harris and the rest of the posse watched the action from a nearby hill. The lawman later shared with newspaper reporters that with each shot Soto fired, he took a step closer to Morse, who was reloading his gun. Sheriff Harris noted that Soto wasn't wearing a hat, and that his hair, which was coal black and very long, blew out on all sides of his uncovered head. It gave him an appearance of something fierce and demonic. Soto had a habit of raising his weapon above his head and bringing his gun swiftly down and firing as the muzzle passed his line of sight. Morse made note of that as he cocked the hammer back on his weapon and shot at the outlaw. The bullet struck the pistol in Soto's hand, disabling it in such a way that the chambers would no longer revolve. It also drove the barrel violently against the desperado's cheek. The shot startled Soto, and he turned and started to run back toward the house. Captain Winchell, who was nearby watching the action, took a flying shot at the outlaw. He missed, the bullet hitting the house.[33]

Morse made a run for his horse and the Henry rifle he'd left behind. He was standing at the northern corner of the corral when Soto reemerged from the house carrying a six-shooter in each hand. He made a mad dash for his horse, which stood saddled and bridled under a nearby tree. Morse called out to the desperado to stop and throw up his hands, but Soto ignored him. Morse had brought his rifle to his shoulder, intending to shoot Soto's horse, when the animal became spooked. He bucked and pulled and broke free of his fastening and dashed away down the canyon.[34]

For a second Soto stood bewildered; then, recovering himself, he turned and ran directly in front of the officer and down the mountain to a point where he had a second horse tethered.[35]

Sheriff Harris raced his horse to the scene, fired at Soto, and missed. Soto was now 150 yards away and was just about to jump on his ride when Morse brought his rifle to his eye and fired, the bullet striking its victim with a sharp click and passing through the outlaw's shoulder.[36]

Stung to desperation by the wound, Soto now abandoned all hope of escape and, turning in his tracks, came right toward the officer. Morse again called out to Soto to throw down his weapon, but appeals to the maddened outlaw were in vain. He continued to charge toward Morse. Recognizing that entreaties were useless and that Soto could not be taken alive, Morse raised his rifle and, taking deliberate aim, sent a bullet crashing through the outlaw's skull.[37]

Harry Morse's duel to the death with Juan Soto remains California's most famous outlaw–lawman gunfight and is considered by historians to be one of the classic shoot-outs of the Old West.

NOTES

Introduction

1. Sheriffs Act, 1887. Section 8, Legislation, United Kingdom.
2. Ibid.
3. *Washington Post*, May 15, 2014.
4. *Oxford English Dictionary*, "posse n. 2, posse comitatus."
5. Michael C. Meyer, *Mexican Rebel: Pascual Orozco and the Mexican Revolution, 1910–1915*, pp. 117–18.
6. *Decatur Herald*, September 1, 1915.
7. *Courier Journal*, September 1, 1915.
8. Hubert H. Bancroft, *History of California: 1860–1890*, p. 204; *Orange County Weekly*, January 8, 2009.
9. Bancroft, *History of California*, pp. 206–7.
10. Ibid., p. 207.
11. Ibid., pp. 208–9; *Los Angeles Times*, December 3, 1968.
12. Bancroft, *History of California*, p. 210.
13. Ibid., pp. 210–11.
14. Ibid.
15. Ibid.; *Sonoma County Journal*, February 6, 1857.
16. Bancroft, *History of California*, pp. 210–11.
17. *Weekly Journal Miner*, June 18, 1919.

18. *Denton Records Chronicle*, February 2, 1864; *Paris News*, April 29, 1998.

19. Sheriffs Act, 1887.

20. *Dodge City and Ford County, Kansas 1870–1920: Pioneer Histories and Stories*, pp. 110–11.

21. *Fort Smith Times*, March 3, 1907.

22. *Daily Ardmoreite*, January 2, 1907.

23. Ibid.

24. Ibid.

25. *Fort Smith Times*, March 3, 1907.

26. *Dodge City Times*, October 5, 1878.

Chapter One: You Haven't Failed until You Quit Trying

1. *Altoona Tribune*, October 20, 1866; *Vermont Daily Transcript*, July 20, 1868.

2. *Courier Journal*, October 16, 1866.

3. Ibid.

4. Ibid.

5. Cleveland Moffett, "The Destruction of the Reno Gang: Stories from the Archives of the Pinkerton Detective Agency," *McClure's Magazine*, 1895. pp. 114–17.

6. Ibid.; *Vermont Daily Transcript*, July 20, 1868.

7. Brant and Fuller, *Reno Gang: History of Jackson County, Indiana*, 1886, pp. 221–29; Cleveland Moffett, *True Detective Stories from the Archives of the Pinkertons*, pp. 549–53.

8. Moffett, "The Destruction of the Reno Gang"; Moffett, *True Detective Stories*, pp. 549–53.

9. Moffett, *True Detective Stories*, pp. 549–53.

10. Brant and Fuller, *Reno Gang*; Moffett, "The Destruction of the Reno Gang"; Moffett, *True Detective Stories*, pp. 549–53.

11. Moffett, "The Destruction of the Reno Gang"; Moffett, *True Detective Stories*, pp. 579–85.

12. Moffett, *True Detective Stories*, pp. 549–53.

13. Ibid.

14. Ibid.

15. Ibid., pp. 565–80.

16. Ibid., pp. 549–53.

17. Ibid.

18. Ibid.

19. Ibid.

20. Ibid.

21. Ibid.

22. Ibid.

23. Ibid.

24. Ibid.

25. Ibid.

26. Ibid.

27. Ibid., pp. 552–59.

28. Ibid., pp. 549–53.

29. Ibid.

30. Moffett, "The Destruction of the Reno Gang"; Moffett, *True Detective Stories*, pp. 549–53; James D. Horan, *The Pinkertons: The Detective Dynasty That Made History*, p. 167.

31. Moffett, *True Detective Stories*, pp. 549–53; Horan, *The Pinkertons*, p. 167.

32. Moffett, "The Destruction of the Reno Gang"; Moffett, *True Detective Stories*, pp. 549–53; *Louisville Daily Courier*, October 27, 1868.

33. *Indianapolis Journal*, December 5, 1868.

34. Moffett, "The Destruction of the Reno Gang"; Moffett, *True Detective Stories*, pp. 553–62.

35. Moffett, *True Detective Stories*, pp. 549–53.

36. Ibid.

37. Moffett, "The Destruction of the Reno Gang"; Moffett, *True Detective Stories*, pp. 554–62; *Tiffin Tribune*, December 14, 1868.

38. Moffett, "The Destruction of the Reno Gang"; Moffett, *True Detective Stories*, pp. 549–53; *Tiffin Tribune*, December 14, 1868.

39. Moffett, "The Destruction of the Reno Gang"; Moffett, *True Detective Stories*, pp. 549–53.

40. Moffett, *True Detective Stories*, pp. 549–53.

41. Ibid.

42. Ibid.

Chapter Two: Surround Yourself with the Best

1. Chris Enss, *Outlaw Tales of California: True Stories of the Golden State's Most Infamous Crooks, Culprits, and Cutthroats*, pp. 1–11.

2. *San Francisco Bulletin*, August 28, 1856.

3. Ibid.

4. Ibid.

5. M. J. Brock and W. B. Lardner, *History of Placer and Nevada Counties*, pp. 374–75.

6. Ibid.

7. Ibid.

8. *San Francisco Bulletin*, August 28, 1856.

9. John Boessenecker, *Badges and Buckshot: Lawlessness in Old California*, pp. 16–19.

10. Ibid.

11. Ibid.

12. Thompson and West, *History of Nevada County, California*, pp. 115–16.

13. Eugene B. Block, *Great Stagecoach Robbers of the West*, p. 79.

14. Thompson and West, *History of Nevada County, California*, pp. 115–16.

15. Ibid.

16. Ibid.

17. Ibid.

18. Ibid.

19. Block, *Great Stagecoach Robbers of the West*, p. 83.

20. *Sacramento Union*, June 3, 1856.

21. *Sacramento Union*, June 9, 1856.

22. Boessenecker, *Badges and Buckshot*, pp. 16–19.

23. *Sonoma County Journal*, October 31, 1856

24. William B. Secrest, *California Badmen: Mean Men with Guns*, pp. 72–73.

25. Ibid.

26. Block, *Great Stagecoach Robbers of the West*, pp. 86–88.

27. *Marysville Express*, September 29, 1856.

28. Ibid.

29. Thompson and West, *History of Nevada County, California*, pp. 115–16.

30. Ibid.

31. Brock and Lardner, *History of Placer and Nevada Counties*, pp. 116–18.

32. Ibid.

33. *Sonoma County Journal*, October 24, 1856

34. Ibid.

35. Ibid.; Block, *Great Stagecoach Robbers of the West*, pp. 88–91.

36. Block, *Great Stagecoach Robbers of the West*, pp. 88–91.

37. Ibid.

38. Ibid.

39. *Sonoma County Journal*, October 24, 1856.

40. *Sonoma County Journal*, October 17, 1856.

41. *Baltimore Sun*, October 30, 1856.

42. *San Francisco Call*, October 5, 1856.

43. Ibid.

Chapter Three: Be Steadfast and Relentless

1. *Coffeyville Weekly Journal*, September 8, 1893.

2. Ibid.

3. Glenn Shirley, *Heck Thomas, Frontier Marshal: The Story of a Real Gunfighter*, pp. 119–26.

4. *Kansas City Gazette*, October 5, 1892.

5. Ibid.

6. *Coffeyville Weekly Journal*, September 8, 1893.

7. Ibid.; *San Francisco Chronicle*, October 7, 1892.

8. *Coffeyville Weekly Journal*, September 8, 1893.

9. Ibid.

10. Ibid.

11. Ibid.

12. *Belle Plaine News*, September 7, 1893.

13. *Columbus Weekly Advocate*, September 7, 1893.

14. Ibid.

15. Shirley, *Heck Thomas, Frontier Marshal*, pp. 15–19.

16. Ibid.

17. Ibid.; *Atlanta Constitution*, April 8, 1892.

18. Floyd Miller, *Bill Tilghman: Marshal of the Last Frontier*, pp. 121–25.

19. Ibid.

20. Ibid.

21. Ibid.

22. Ibid., pp. 126–29.

23. Ibid., pp. 138–41.

24. Ibid.

25. Ibid.

26. Ibid., pp. 119–76.

27. Ibid.

28. *King City Chronicle*, June 15, 1894.

29. Ibid.

30. Ibid.

31. Miller, *Bill Tilghman*, pp. 136–40.

32. Ibid.

33. Ibid.

34. Ibid., pp. 131–33.

35. Ibid.

36. Ibid.

37. Ibid.

38. Ibid.

39. Ibid.

40. *Evening Times*, September 3, 1895.

41. *Evening Gazette*, August 21, 1895.

42. Miller, *Bill Tilghman*, pp. 162–64.

43. Ibid.

44. *Weekly Republican-Traveler*, January 23, 1896.

45. Miller, *Bill Tilghman*, pp. 171–75.

46. *Jefferson Gazette*, July 9, 1896.

47. Miller, *Bill Tilghman*, pp. 156–57.

48. Ibid.

49. Ibid.

50. *Kansas City Journal*, August 26, 1896.

51. Miller, *Bill Tilghman*, pp. 156–57.

Chapter Four: Create a Strategic Road Map

1. Howard Kazanjian and Chris Enss, *Thunder Over the Prairie: The True Story of a Murder and a Manhunt by the Greatest Posse of All Time*, pp. 1–4.

2. *Ford County Globe*, October 8, 1878; Stanley Vestal, *Queen of Cowtowns: Killing of Dora Hand*, p. 162; Charles C. Lowther, *Dodge City, Kansas*, p. 106.

3. Earle Forrest, *Dora Hand: The Dance Hall Singer of Old Dodge City*, p. 14.

4. Lowther, *Dodge City, Kansas*, p. 177.

5. Kazanjian and Enss, *Thunder Over the Prairie*, p. 10.

6. Fannie Garretson, Letter to Messrs. Esher, October 5, 1878.

7. Vestal, *Queen of Cowtowns*, p. 162.

8. Samuel Carter III, *Cowboy Capital of the World: The Saga of Dodge City*, p. 124.

9. Lowther, *Dodge City, Kansas*, p. 182.

10. Kazanjian and Enss, *Thunder Over the Prairie*, p. 27.

11. *Dodge City Times*, October 12, 1878.

12. Nyle Miller and Joseph Snell, *Great Gunfighters of the Kansas Cowtowns*, p. 232.

13. *Dodge City Times*, October 12, 1878.

14. Ibid.

15. Kazanjian and Enss, *Thunder Over the Prairie*, pp. 52–56.

16. Stuart N. Lake, *Wyatt Earp: Frontier Marshall*, p. 29.

17. Kazanjian and Enss, *Thunder Over the Prairie*, pp. 92–97.

18. Ibid.

19. Ibid.

20. Ibid.

21. *Dodge City Times*, October 12, 1878.

22. Lake, *Wyatt Earp*, p. 29.

23. Lowther, *Dodge City, Kansas*, p. 175.

24. Floyd Miller, *Bill Tilghman: Marshal of the Last Frontier*, p. 142.

25. Robert K. DeArment, *Bat Masterson: The Man and the Legend*, p. 123.

26. Vestal, *Queen of Cowtowns*, p. 6.

27. Allen Barra, *Inventing Wyatt Earp: His Life and Many Legends*, p. 86; Casey Tefertiller, *Wyatt Earp: The Life Behind the Legend*, pp. 217–19.

28. Tefertiller, *Wyatt Earp*, pp. 86, 217–19.

29. Lowther, *Dodge City, Kansas*, p. 175.

30. Kazanjian and Enss, *Thunder Over the Prairie*, pp. 100–103.

31. *Dodge City Times*, October 12, 1878.

32. Kazanjian and Enss, *Thunder Over the Prairie*, pp. 105–7.

33. Miller and Snell, *Great Gunfighters of the Kansas Cowtowns*, p. 235.

34. Kazanjian and Enss, *Thunder Over the Prairie*, pp. 110–12.

35. Ibid.

36. Barra, *Inventing Wyatt Earp*, p. 86.

37. *Dodge City Times*, October 29, 1878.

38. Carter, *Cowboy Capital of the World*, p. 126.

39. Barra, *Inventing Wyatt Earp*, p. 86.

40. *Dodge City Times*, May 10, 1879.

41. *Dodge City Times*, May 24, 1879.

42. Kazanjian and Enss, *Thunder Over the Prairie*, pp. 117–25.

43. Ibid.

44. *Ford County Globe*, December 10, 1878.

45. *Ford County Globe*, March 18, 1879.

46. Kazanjian and Enss, *Thunder Over the Prairie*, pp. 117–25.

47. *Dodge City Times*, January 11, 1879.

48. Miller and Snell, *Great Gunfighters of the Kansas Cowtowns*, p. 31.

49. Miller, *Bill Tilghman*, p. 82.

50. Kazanjian and Enss, *Thunder Over the Prairie*, pp. 117–25.

51. *Dodge City Times*, January 25, 1879.

Chapter Five: Always Plan for Setbacks

1. Chris Enss, *Outlaw Tales of California*, pp. 12–14.
2. Robert Greenwood, *The California Outlaw: Tiburcio Vasquez*, pp. 31–34.
3. Ibid.
4. Ibid.
5. Ibid.
6. Ibid.
7. Ibid.
8. Enss, *Outlaw Tales of California*, pp. 13–17.
9. *Daily Signal*, April 19, 1905; Greenwood, *The California Outlaw*, pp. 14–16.
10. Greenwood, *The California Outlaw*, pp. 21–23.
11. Ibid.
12. Ibid., pp. 16–18.
13. Ibid.
14. Ibid.
15. Ibid., 22–26.
16. Ibid.
17. Ibid.
18. Ibid., pp. 73–78.
19. Ibid.
20. Ibid.
21. Ibid.
22. Ibid.
23. John Boessenecker, *Bandido: The Life and Times of Tiburcio Vasquez*, pp. 278–82.
24. Ibid.
25. Ibid., pp. 151–56.
26. Ibid., pp. 162–70.

27. Ibid.

28. Ibid.

29. Ibid., pp. 174–78.

30. Ibid.

31. George Beers, *Vasquez and the Hunted Bandits of San Joaquin*, pp. 182–86.

32. Ibid.

33. Ibid.

34. Ibid.

35. Ibid.

36. Greenwood, *The California Outlaw*, pp. 218–20.

37. Ibid.

38. Ibid.

39. Beers, *Vasquez and the Hunted Bandits*, pp. 216–20.

40. Ibid.

41. Ibid., pp. 240–46.

42. Ibid.

43. Ibid.

44. Ibid., pp. 227–29.

45. Ibid.

46. Ibid.

47. Ibid., pp. 231–33.

48. Ibid.

49. Ibid.

50. Ibid.

51. Ibid.

52. *Los Angeles Herald*, July 28, 1874.

53. Beers, *Vasquez and the Hunted Bandits*, pp. 236–40.

54. Ibid.

55. Ibid.

56. Ibid.

57. Ibid.

58. Ibid.

59. Ibid., pp. 257–64.

60. Ibid.

61. Ibid.

62. Ibid.

63. Ibid.

64. Ibid.

65. Ibid., pp. 273–76.

66. Ibid.

67. Ibid.

68. Ibid., p. 293.

Chapter Six: It's Okay to Regroup and Reflect

1. Richard Reinhardt, *Out West on the Overland Trail*, p. 44.

2. *Life and Adventures of Sam Bass: The Notorious Union Pacific and Texas Train Robber*, pp. 13–15.

3. Ibid.

4. Ibid.

5. Ibid.

6. *Indianapolis News*, September 19, 1877.

7. *Life and Adventures of Sam Bass*, pp. 1–5.

8. Ibid.

9. *Life and Adventures of Sam Bass*, pp. 3–7.

10. Ibid.

11. *Life and Adventures of Sam Bass*, pp. 8–11.

12. Ibid., pp. 12–16.

13. Ibid.

14. Ibid.

15. Ibid.

16. Ibid., pp. 20–23.

17. Ibid.

18. Ibid.

19. *Mexico Weekly Ledger*, October 18, 1877.

20. *Life and Adventures of Sam Bass*, pp. 20–23.

21. Ibid.

22. Ibid., pp. 24–26.

23. Ibid.

24. Ibid., pp. 26–28.

25. Ibid.

26. Ibid.

27. Ibid.

28. *Dallas Weekly Herald*, April 13, 1878.

29. Ibid.

30. *Life and Adventures of Sam Bass*, pp. 28–31.

31. Ibid.

32. *Dallas Weekly Herald*, April 13, 1878.

33. *Life and Adventures of Sam Bass*, pp. 31–38.

34. Ibid.

35. *The Times*, June 9, 1878.

36. *Life and Adventures of Sam Bass*, pp. 31–38.

37. Ibid., pp. 38–45.

38. Ibid., pp. 55–64.

39. Ibid.

40. Ibid.

41. Ibid., pp. 65–71.

42. Ibid.

43. Ibid.

44. *San Marcos Free Press*, September 14, 1878.

45. Ibid.

46. Ibid.

47. Ibid.

48. *Life and Adventures of Sam Bass*, pp. 65–72.

49. Ibid.

50. Ibid., pp. 77–86.

51. Ibid.

52. Ibid.

53. Ibid.

54. Ibid., pp. 86–89.

55. Ibid.

Chapter Seven: Do What Has to Be Done

1. *Valley Morning Star*, October 24, 1948.

2. Ibid.

3. J. Evetts Haley, *Jeff Milton: A Good Man with a Gun*, pp. 267–68.

4. Ibid.

5. Karen Tanner and John D. Tanner, *The Bronco Bill Gang*, pp. 12–13.

6. Haley, *Jeff Milton*, pp. 31–35.

7. Ibid.

8. Ibid.

9. Ibid., pp. 266–67.

10. Tanner and Tanner, *The Bronco Bill Gang*, pp. 28–29.

11. Ibid., pp. 41–42.

12. Ibid.

13. Ibid.

14. Ibid.

15. *Albuquerque Citizen*, March 29, 1898.

16. Haley, *Jeff Milton*, pp. 290–94.

17. Ibid.

18. Ibid.

19. *Albuquerque Citizen*, May 26, 1898.

20. Ibid.

21. Ibid.

22. Ibid.

23. Haley, *Jeff Milton*, pp. 233–35.

24. Ibid.

25. *Arizona Republic*, July 25, 1898.

26. Haley, *Jeff Milton*, pp. 296–301.

27. Ibid.

28. Ibid.

29. Ibid.

30. Ibid.

31. Ibid.

32. Ibid.; *Los Angeles Herald*, August 29, 1898.

33. *Los Angeles Herald*, August 29, 1898.

34. Ibid.

35. *Los Angeles Herald*, August 29, 1898.

36. Ibid.

37. Ibid.

38. Haley, *Jeff Milton*, pp. 336–41.

39. Ibid.

Chapter Eight: Accept Success with Humility and Gratitude

1. George Beers, *Vasquez and the Hunted Bandits of San Joaquin*, pp. 151–70.

2. Ibid.

3. Ibid.

4. Ibid.

5. *San Francisco Chronicle*, April 10, 1871.

6. *Los Angeles Times*, July 12, 1925.

7. Ibid.; Enss, *Outlaw Tales of California*, pp. 34–38.

8. Enss, *Outlaw Tales of California*, pp. 34–38.

9. Beers, *Vasquez and the Hunted Bandits*, pp. 151–70.

10. Ibid.

11. Ibid.

12. Ibid.

13. Ibid.; Jay Nash, *Encyclopedia of Western Lawmen and Outlaws*, p. 289.

14. Beers, *Vasquez and the Hunted Bandits*, pp. 151–70.

15. Ibid.

16. Ibid.

17. Ibid.

18. *Cincinnati Enquirer*, August 18, 1888.

19. Ibid.

20. Ibid.

21. Ibid.

22. Ibid.

23. *Oakland Daily Evening Tribune*, September 1, 1888.

24. Ibid.

25. Ibid.

26. Ibid.

27. Ibid.

28. Ibid.

29. Ibid.

30. Ibid.

31. Ibid.

32. Ibid.

33. Ibid.

34. Ibid.
35. Ibid.
36. Ibid.
37. Ibid.

BIBLIOGRAPHY

Bancroft, Hubert H. *History of California: 1860–1890*. Charleston, SC: Nabu Press / BiblioLife, 2014.

Barra, Allen. *Inventing Wyatt Earp: His Life and Many Legends*. New York: Carroll & Graf, 1998.

Beers, George. *Vasquez and the Hunted Bandits of the San Joaquin*. New York: Robert M. De Witt, Publisher, 1875.

Block, Eugene B. *Great Stagecoach Robbers of the West*. New York: Doubleday, 1962.

Boessenecker, John. *Badges and Buckshot: Lawlessness in Old California*. Norman: University of Oklahoma Press, 1993.

———. *Lawman: The Life and Times of Harry Morse*. Norman: University of Oklahoma Press, 1998.

———. *Bandido: The Life and Times of Tiburcio Vasquez*. Norman: University of Oklahoma Press, 2014.

Braddock, Betty, and Jeanie Covalt. *Dodge City*. Dodge City: Kansas Heritage Center, 1982.

Brock, M. J., and W. B. Lardner. *History of Placer and Nevada Counties*. Los Angeles: Historic Record Company, 1924.

Carter, Samuel III. *Cowboy Capital of the World: The Saga of Dodge City*. Garden City, NY: Doubleday, 1973.

DeArment, Robert K. *Bat Masterson: The Man and the Legend*. Norman: University of Oklahoma Press, 1979.

Enss, Chris. *Outlaw Tales of California: True Stories of the Golden State's Most Infamous Crooks, Culprits, and Cutthroats.* Guilford, CT: TwoDot, 2013.

Greenwood, Robert. *The California Outlaw: Tiburcio Vasquez.* Los Gatos, CA: The Talisman Press, 1960.

Haley, J. Evetts. *Jeff Milton: A Good Man with a Gun.* Norman: University of Oklahoma Press, 1948.

Horan, James D. *The Pinkertons: The Detective Dynasty That Made History.* New York: Bonanza Books, 1967.

Kazanjian, Howard, and Chris Enss. *Thunder Over the Prairie: The True Story of a Murder and a Manhunt by the Greatest Posse of All Time.* Guilford, CT: TwoDot, 2009.

Lake, Stuart N. *Wyatt Earp: Frontier Marshal.* New York: Pocket Books, 1931.

Lowther, Charles C. *Dodge City, Kansas.* Philadelphia: Dorrance, 1940.

MacDonald, Franklin. *Eight Weeks to Sundown.* San Francisco: Pacific Bell, 1984.

Masterson, W. B. *Famous Gunfighters of the Western Frontier.* Houston: Frontier Press of Texas, 1907.

Meyer, Michael C. *Mexican Rebel: Pascual Orozco and the Mexican Revolution, 1910–1915.* Lincoln: University of Nebraska Press, 1967.

Miller, Floyd. *Bill Tilghman: Marshal of the Last Frontier.* New York: Doubleday, 1968.

Miller, Nyle, and Joseph Snell. *Great Gunfighters of the Kansas Cowtowns.* Lincoln: University of Nebraska Press, 1963.

Moffett, Cleveland. *True Detective Stories from the Archives of the Pinkertons.* New York: G. W. Dillingham, 1897.

Morn, Frank. *The Eye that Never Sleeps: A History of the Pinkerton National Detective Agency.* Bloomington: Indiana University Press, 1982.

Nash, Jay R. *Encyclopedia of Western Lawmen and Outlaws.* New York: Paragon House, 1989.

Reinhardt, Richard. *Out West on the Overland Trail.* Sanger, CA: American West Publishing, 1967.

Secrest, William B. *Perilous Trails, Dangerous Men: Early California Stage-coach Robbers and Their Desperate Careers.* Clovis, CA: Word Dancer Press, 2002.

———. *California Badmen: Mean Men with Guns.* Clovis, CA: Word Dancer Press, 2006.

Shirley, Glenn. *Heck Thomas, Frontier Marshal: The Story of a Real Gunfighter.* New York: Chilton, 1962.

Tanner, Karen, and John D. Tanner. *The Bronco Bill Gang.* Norman: University of Oklahoma, 2011.

Tefertiller, Casey. *Wyatt Earp: The Life Behind the Legend.* New York: John Wiley & Sons, 1997.

Vestal, Stanley. *Queen of Cowtowns: Killing of Dora Hand.* New York: Harper & Brothers, 1952.

Newspapers

Albuquerque Citizen, Albuquerque, New Mexico, March 29, 1898.

———. Albuquerque, New Mexico, May 26, 1898.

Altoona Tribune, Altoona, Pennsylvania, July 20, 1868.

———. Blair County, Pennsylvania, October 20, 1866.

Arizona Republic, Phoenix, Arizona, July 25, 1898.

Arkansas City Daily Traveler, Arkansas City, Kansas, March 12, 1892.

Atlanta Constitution, Atlanta, Georgia, April 8, 1892.

Baltimore Sun, Baltimore, Maryland, October 30, 1856.

Belle Plaine News, Belle Plaine, Minnesota, September 7, 1893.

Cincinnati Enquirer, Cincinnati, Ohio, August 18, 1888.

Coffeyville Weekly Journal, Coffeyville, Kansas, September 8, 1893.

Columbus Weekly Advocate, Columbus, Kansas, September 7, 1893.

Courier Journal, Louisville, Kentucky, October 16, 1866.

———. Louisville, Kentucky, September 1, 1915.

Daily Ardmoreite, Ardmore, Oklahoma, January 2, 1907.

Daily Ohio Statesman, Columbus, Ohio, August 15, 1868.

Daily Signal, Crowley, Louisiana, April 19, 1905.

Dallas Weekly Herald, Dallas, Texas, April 13, 1878.

Decatur Herald, Decatur, Illinois, September 1, 1915.

Denton Records Chronicle, Denton, Texas, February 2, 1864.

Dodge City Times, Dodge City, Kansas, October 5, 1878.

———. Dodge City, Kansas, October 12, 1878.

———. Dodge City, Kansas, October 29, 1878.

———. Dodge City, Kansas, January 11, 1879.

———. Dodge City, Kansas, January 25, 1879.

———. Dodge City, Kansas, May 10, 1879.

———. Dodge City, Kansas, May 24, 1879.

Evening Gazette, Cedar Rapids, Iowa, August 21, 1895.

Evening Times, Ada, Oklahoma, September 3, 1895.

Ford County Globe, Dodge City, Kansas, October 8, 1878.

———. Dodge City, Kansas, December 10, 1878.

———. Dodge City, Kansas, March 18, 1879.

Fort Scott Daily Monitor, Fort Scott, Kansas, July 23, 1878.

Fort Smith Times, Fort Smith, Arkansas, February 6, 1857.

———. Fort Smith, Arkansas, March 3, 1907.

Fremont Weekly Journal, Fremont, Ohio, December 18, 1868.

Indianapolis Journal, Indianapolis, Indiana, December 5, 1868.

Indianapolis News, Indianapolis, Indiana, September 19, 1877.

Jackson County Banner, Brownstown, Indiana, April 10, 1976.

Jefferson Gazette, Jefferson, Ohio, July 9, 1896.

Kansas City Gazette, Kansas City, Missouri, October 5, 1892.

Kansas City Journal, Kansas City, Missouri, August 26, 1896.

King City Chronicle, King City, Missouri, June 15, 1894.

Leavenworth Times, Leavenworth, Kansas, June 9, 1894.

Los Angeles Herald, Los Angeles, California, May 15, 1874.

———. Los Angeles, California, July 28, 1874.

———. Los Angeles, California, August 29, 1898.

Los Angeles Times, Los Angeles, California, July 12, 1925.

———. Los Angeles, California, December 3, 1968.

Louisiana Democrat, Alexandria, Louisiana, June 21, 1871.

Louisville Daily Courier, Louisville, Kentucky, October 27, 1868.

Marysville Express, Marysville, California, September 29, 1856.

Memphis Daily Appeal, Memphis, Tennessee, July 27, 1878.

Mexico Weekly Ledger, Mexico, Missouri, October 18, 1877.

New North-West, Deer Lodge, Montana, May 30, 1874.

Oakland Daily Evening Tribune, Oakland, California, September 1, 1888.

Oakland Tribune, Oakland, California, July 27, 1941.

Orange County Weekly, Orange County, California, January 8, 2009.

Paris News, Paris, Texas, April 29, 1998.

Raleigh News, Raleigh, North Carolina, May 29, 1874.

Record Union, Sacramento, California, January 15, 1880.

Sacramento Union, Sacramento, California, June 3, 1856.

———. Sacramento, California, June 9, 1856.

San Francisco Bulletin, San Francisco, California, August 28, 1856.

San Francisco Call, San Francisco, California, October 5, 1856.

———. San Francisco, California, October 14, 1900.

San Francisco Chronicle, San Francisco, California, April 10, 1871.

———. San Francisco, California, May 15, 1874.

———. San Francisco, California, October 7, 1892.

San Marcos Free Press, San Marcos, Texas, September 14, 1878.

Santa Cruz Sentinel, Santa Cruz, California, March 6, 1945.

Santa Cruz Weekly Sentinel, Santa Cruz, California, November 8, 1873.

Semi-Weekly Wisconsin, Milwaukee, Wisconsin, December 19, 1868.

Sonoma County Journal, Petaluma, California, October 10, 1856.

———. Petaluma, California, October 17, 1856.

———. Petaluma, California, October 24, 1856.

———. Petaluma, California, October 31, 1856.

———. Petaluma, California, February 6, 1857.

The Tennessean, Nashville, Tennessee, July 26, 1868.

———. Nashville, Tennessee, August 1, 1868.

———. Nashville, Tennessee, August 12, 1868.

———. Nashville, Tennessee, May 28, 1871.

Terre Haute Tribune, Terre Haute, Indiana, March 30, 1961.

Tiffin Tribune, Tiffin, Ohio, December 14, 1868.

———. Tiffin, Ohio, December 24, 1868.

The Times, Shreveport, Louisiana, June 9, 1878.

Tri-Weekly Commercial, Wilmington, North Carolina, November 22, 1856.

Valley Morning Star, Harlingen, Texas, October 24, 1948.

Vermont Daily Transcript, Saint Albans, Vermont, July 20, 1868.

Washington Post, Washington, DC, May 15, 2014.

Weekly Journal Miner, Prescott, Arizona, June 18, 1919.

Weekly Republican-Traveler, Arkansas City, Kansas, January 23, 1896.

Wichita Daily Eagle, Wichita, Kansas, September 5, 1893.

———. Wichita, Kansas, July 21, 1907.

Correspondence/Newsletters/Pamphlets/Periodicals

Beer, George. "The Taking of Tiburcio Vasquez," *Six-Guns and Saddle Leather: A Bibliography of Books and Pamphlets*, No. 89, 1875.

Brant and Fuller. *Reno Gang: History of Jackson County, Indiana*. Jackson County Historical Society, 1886.

Dodge City and Ford County, Kansas 1870–1920: Pioneer Histories and Stories. Ford County Historical Society, Dodge City, Kansas, 1996.

Forrest, Earle. *Dora Hand: The Dance Hall Singer of Old Dodge City. Los Angeles Corral Newsletter*, No. 7, 1957.

Garretson, Fannie. Letter to Messrs. Esher, October 5, 1878.

Life and Adventures of Sam Bass: The Notorious Union Pacific and Texas Train Robber. Dallas, TX: Dallas Commercial Stream Print, 1878.

Moffett, Cleveland. "The Destruction of the Reno Gang: Stories from the Archives of the Pinkerton Detective Agency," *McClure's Magazine*, 1895.

Pinkerton, William. "Highway of the Railroad," *North American Review*, Vol. 0157, Issue 444, November 1893.

Sheriffs Act, 1887. Section 8, Legislation, United Kingdom. Eyre & Spottis-
woode, Printers to the Queen's Most Excellent Majesty.

Thompson and West. *History of Nevada County, California.* Berkeley, CA:
Howell-North Books, 1880.

INDEX

ABOUT THE AUTHOR

Chris Enss is an author, scriptwriter, and comedienne who has written for television and film and performed on cruise ships and onstage. She has worked with award-winning musicians, writers, directors, producers, and as a screenwriter for Tricor Entertainment, but her passion is telling the stories of the men and women who shaped the history and mythology of the American West. Some of the most famous names in history, not to mention film and popular culture, populate her books. She's written or cowritten more than two dozen books for TwoDot. And she's also a licensed private detective.